Purpose, Incorporated

Turning Cause Into Your Competitive Advantage

John Wood and Amalia McGibbon

Contents

Preface

Greetings from Nepal! I am writing this in front of a roaring fireplace in a tiny guesthouse nearly ten thousand feet above sea level. I'm here in a remote section of the Himalayas because seventeen years ago I founded a charity called Room to Read, and our work allows me to visit some of the thousands of schools and libraries we're supporting. Those travels take me to exotic locations, including fishing villages in the Mekong Delta, Syrian refugee camps in Jordan, and coastal villages in Sri Lanka rebuilding after the thirty-plus-year civil war.

Tonight, I'm proud to be putting the finishing touches on my third business book—this one focusing on how companies can pursue both purpose and profit simultaneously and build better businesses as a result. But all this may cause you to wonder, why is a full-time do-gooder writing business books?

Well, first off, because my work didn't always take me up into the mountains. Early in my career, I was a senior Microsoft executive who spent most of his time thinking about the company's hard-nosed business goals: how to launch new products, outflank competitors to capture market share, and open new subsidiaries. Truth be told, I was also paying a lot of attention to feathering my nest with as many stock options as possible.

In 1998, to celebrate my seven-year anniversary with the company, I set out on a bold adventure: an eighteen-day, two-hundred-mile trek in Nepal's Annapurna mountain range. At the end of an arduous first day, I sat down in a teahouse and soon met the headmaster of the local school. He offered to give me a quick tour of the dilapidated school, ending in a library that was completely devoid of children's books.

Pointing to the empty shelves, he explained, "In Nepal, we are too poor to afford education. But until we have education, we will always remain poor." As I wondered what I could do to help, the headmaster gave me a homework assignment: "Perhaps, sir, you will someday come back with books."

Rebooting My Life

On my flight back home to sunny Sydney, I composed an email appeal to friends, coworkers, and family: "Please, help me set up a library in Bahundanda. Send me your used children's books! *Clifford the Big Red Dog*, *The Cat in the Hat*, *Goodnight Moon*—whatever you've got!" The response was overwhelming, and within a year my seventy-three-year-old retired father was helping me figure out how to get three thousand donated books to that little village. The solution would involve a father-son adventure trip, six rented donkeys, and the happiest day of my life.

As we unloaded our treasure, it was like a mosh pit as the eager young students grabbed the first brightly colored children's books they had ever seen. I will never forget the kids laughing as they saw an octopus for the first time—or the little girl who asked, "Mister, what does the ocean taste like?" And on that day, at the age of thirty-five—thinking about my job at Microsoft and my desire to have an impact on something other than my bank account—I made the rather insane decision to leave a lucrative career and start a nonprofit to bring books and literacy to children across the poorest parts of the world.

It was rather nerve-racking to walk into my boss's office to utter those epic words: "Sorry, but I'm quitting!"—especially since I was not doing something logical and predictable, like moving on to a different tech company. Instead, I was going to invent a new future, one that would have me hiring yaks in addition to those rented donkeys to go even higher into the Himalayas.

It's tough to get a new charity off the ground. On many days, it sucked. We had no fund-raising experience and zero brand recognition, and during the first few months, I was the only donor. But we ended up hitting not just one tipping point but several and have become the most far-reaching and effective education NGO working in the developing world. Our teams have sponsored the construction of twenty-five hundred school buildings, funded long-term scholarships for over fifty thousand young women, and trained over fifteen thousand teachers in literacy and library instruction. That first little library in Bahundanda has multiplied beyond my wildest dreams; today over twenty thousand communities in fifteen countries have Room to Read libraries. Over twelve million students have access to enhanced educational opportunities, and that number will grow to over fifteen million during the next year.

People often ask me about the keys to our success. One was that from the beginning, our founding team vowed to run the organization like a business. Too many charities are chaotically run and are long on heart but short on actual results. We vowed to be different: we'd have a strategic plan, tight financials, KPIs, dashboards, and unapologetic culling of nonperformers. We'd hire "corporate refugees" who had cut their teeth in the private sector and were now willing to devote the next stage of their careers to building a global education movement. That focus helped to get us off the ground, but something even bigger was brewing. Tectonic plates were starting to shift. And that would be critical to taking Room to Read to serious scale.

Where Cause Meets Capitalism

As our team continued to grow, we met more and more business leaders who expressed a desire to work with us. Many had originally come on board as individual donors after attending fund-raising events, only later to ask, "How can I get my company involved?" Through hours of conversations with hundreds of business professionals, we learned that many companies were in the early stages of a transition. Where they'd once had a siloed corporate social responsibility department, they were now trying to infuse wide swaths of their companies with the mantra of purpose. Many were rejecting the notion that good works were antithetical to profits and instead were finding ways to align purpose with business goals, including building bonds with customers, generating positive buzz on social media, recruiting millennials, increasing motivation, and lowering attrition rates for their best employees.

We talked to a wide range of companies—from unknown start-ups in fields as varied as skin care and bottled water to pre-IPO tech companies to household names like Google and Starbucks. While in many ways different, each shared a common trait: they had found ways to stand for something bigger than just themselves. Yes, they cared about sales and net income and market share, because if they didn't get those right, then they wouldn't be in business. But the key was that these weren't the only things they cared about. They dared to talk about having a bigger mission, one focused on social change, fixing long-standing problems, and providing uplift for the world's poorest people. These business leaders saw purpose not as a nice thing to do but as a must-do—a key competitive advantage that could enhance enterprise value.

It is to help explain, celebrate, and accelerate this shift that I decided to write this book. To be clear, I'm challenging myself as an author, and you as the reader, to remain in hard-core capitalist mode, rather than focus on the obvious feel-good factor. I will provide examples of many companies that are using purpose as a competitive advantage and a way to improve the world. I hope this book can be a clarion call to encourage people at all levels of their companies to create their own unique marriage between cause and capitalism. To help, I'll provide dozens of illuminating examples of how they've made it happen. As I've interviewed CEOs and interns, enthusiastic customers, and wary investors, I've learned that the corporate world is not what it once was. There's a new land of opportunity, and—luckily for all—its streets are paved with purpose.

1

When Purpose Meets Profitability

While still in its early days, the move toward incorporating purpose into the values and business models of companies is an encouraging sign. I believe it shows that we're finally leaving behind one of the most shortsighted and ill-advised falsehoods in corporate history: that purpose and profits are somehow antithetical.

A major strain of free-market American capitalism has opposed the role of purpose in business for more than 150 years. For example, when the Ford Motor Company announced in 1914 that it would try to help its workers move into the middle class by doubling their wages to five dollars per day, the *Wall Street Journal* declared that the act was tantamount to applying "biblical or spiritual principles into a field where they do not belong." It sternly admonished Ford, saying that "in his social endeavor," he "has committed economic blunders, if not crimes."

In the history of business, there has been a strong bias toward clearly separating purpose and profitability. Purpose was a do-gooding activity best left to governments and the social sector. Business leaders, meanwhile, would pursue profits and then more profits, with the paramount goal of maximizing returns to shareholders.

One of the people we must thank for this legacy is Milton Friedman. I first heard of Friedman when, as a student at the Kellogg Business School, I asked a professor if, as a future executive, I could think beyond profits and integrate some measure of social good into my career. He responded by quoting Friedman: "There is one and only one social responsibility of business—to use its resources and engage in activities designed to increase its profits."

But Friedman was wrong then and even more wrong now. Customers demand more accountability from the businesses that produce goods and services, and more businesses are beginning to embrace the economics of doing things right the first time, rather than settling lawsuits, facing prosecution, and paying fines when their culture produces corner cutting and a "what you can get away with" approach to issues such as global warming, clean water, labor standards, and education. The clear lines of delineation between for-profits and nonprofits have begun to blur. While the charity world used to attract leaders who were often long on heart but short on organizational skills, donors and boards are demanding these organizations be run in a more businesslike manner. They want to see competent level-one leadership, bold and clear goals, data-driven results, and low overhead ratios.

I spoke about this with Michael Thatcher, the president and CEO of Charity Navigator, and he pointed out that Charity Navigator's very existence is the result of donors demanding greater accountability and transparency from nonprofits, as well as more businesslike behaviors within the sector. Charity Navigator is America's largest independent evaluator of the nonprofit sector, having rated over nine thousand of the nation's largest and best-known charities. In the last five years, it's noted a positive trend in the ratings results, showing a 10 percent increase in the number of three- and four-star-rated charities (four is the highest rating).

Take Charity Water, a nonprofit whose software is the envy of some for-profit companies. Its leading-edge donation platform makes it not just easier than ever for users to donate and fund-raise but also boasts an accountability engine that nobody had ever seen before, which tracks every dollar into the field. So, eighteen to twenty-four months after a person donates money, he or she will get an email that says, "Your money went to *this* well, in *this* community, and here's the photo of the ribbon-cutting." The charity's software-driven approach complements its storytelling and has attracted employees from the tech world, including one-time CTO Greg Pass, formerly the CTO at Twitter.

Meanwhile, companies around the globe are increasingly falling over themselves to declare their commitment to sustainable development. They hear demands from their customers, employees, and government regulators to run themselves in ways that are ethical and positive for society. Industrial giant GE's home appliances are engineered from the ground up to save energy and energy dollars. Parking lots are regularly outfitted for the growing numbers of all-electric cars from the big US carmakers, the same people who killed the local trolley one hundred years ago as well as earlier incarnations of cars that didn't guzzle fossil fuel. Walmart, the bête noire of liberal capitalism, now carries organic produce. And on and on.

That's what I call the blurring of the lines. Nonprofits are adopting the best of the business world, while business leaders are finding a way for their companies to defy Professor Friedman and to pursue outcomes that are about more than just the bottom line. Once upon a time, the intersection on the Venn diagram of purpose and profitability was small enough to require a magnifying glass. Today, it is growing radically in size.

Why Now?

We live in an era marked by disintegrating trust in the institutions on which our society was once built: business, government, and organized religion. People's faith in these institutions to solve problems has been rocked by scandals, unethical behavior, and a continued inability to solve big problems. As a result, there is an intense search for a better way.

The business world got another black eye from the global financial crisis, as we once again learned what can happen when profits are viewed as the holy grail and the most meaningful yardstick of success. But many companies have pivoted as executives have begun to listen to the demands of their customers and employees to be part of the solution rather than part of the problem. They have learned, through record fines, legal bills, and loss of customers, that there can be a substantial cost to having their sole focus be on profits.

This has occurred while people around the world are losing confidence in government. It's happening across all political affiliations and stripes. In the United States, congressional approval ratings for both parties have been abysmally low for over a decade, and Donald Trump has the lowest first-term approval ratings of any president in history. We've seen Brexit in the UK and the overthrow of governments from Tunisia to Egypt. Across the globe, many are searching for that mythical "outsider" who can shake up the system.

This urgency is also dialed up by persistent and growing income inequality. The top 1 percent continues to gain more and more of the income growth in the United States, while everyone else has been left behind. The economist Mohamed El-Erian estimates that in the United States, the richest 1 percent managed to capture 95 percent of the income gains since the 2008 global financial crisis. The top tenth of that 1 percent owns a remarkable 22 percent of the wealth. Meanwhile, middle-income household growth has stagnated or declined, while health-care and education costs have seen consistent annual increases in the double digits. The 1 percent may see their comfortable worlds crumble if they don't help to address the inequality that helped them reach their current stations.

Finally, ubiquitous and constantly connected social-media platforms are now an unpredictable force of public opinion that can explode an issue like wildfire. From the concerned mother who took down Mylan over price gouging on the EpiPen to the Tunisian fruit vendor who protested endemic corruption and brought down a government, the hyperconnected world offers numerous ways to promote social change. Millions now use these as platforms to praise those companies they perceive as socially responsible and to slam those who aren't. Of course, social media's ability to create instant influence and spread simple messages also leverages destructive and angry forces and gives dangerous people a louder voice.

Overall, these factors have accelerated the marriage of cause and capitalism. Businesses realize their customers will reward them if they bridge the void between capitalism and cause with products and services that promote widely shared values that improve the quality of life for a society.

Still, the potential for momentum at many well-meaning companies is deterred by what I refer to as purpose inhibitors.

Purpose Inhibitors: Shackling the Buzz

Our research and interviews for the book make it clear that many companies with good intentions are stuck, and they don't know how to get unstuck. We must know the enemy to fight it, so let's briefly review the inhibitors here, with a plan to cover them in depth later in the book:

- Many leaders have bought into a false dichotomy, believing that if they are doing good for their community or the world, this must somehow be deleterious to their profitability. They see only the either-or and therefore miss the opportunity to conceive of a world in which they could have both. When someone proposes a purpose-driven initiative, their first instinct may be to respond, "We can't afford this!" In their minds, there is a serious risk of "giving away the store."

- For every company you know that made the journey, there's another one hunkering down, hoping this is a phase that will pass. Purpose, they hope, is just a fad they see on the cover of business magazines. "Meanwhile, please excuse me, but I will just stick my head back in the sand."

- Many executives see it as merely a nice-to-have or as something that can be siloed, with a single employee or a Corporate Social Responsibility (CSR) department stuck in a tower (like Rapunzel) to spend the days churning out puffed-up press releases that no one will read or believe. One CEO I interviewed told me, "If your response to *purpose* is to say you have a CSR department, that means you're reducing this to a box-ticking exercise."

- Other companies talk about it, but they don't *mean it*. Remember those advertisements Volkswagen ran bragging about their sustainability rankings, only to have it all unravel once its diesel-emissions cheating was revealed to the world? How in the aftermath of police killings in America and Black Lives Matter marches, the reaction from Pepsi was to put out their widely disparaged Kendall Jenner video? Those companies now, thank goodness, get called out faster than ever (and in Pepsi's case were quick to admit it and apologize). And yet...so many keep trying to game the system.

- Many people I interviewed told me similar variations on the same theme: "I know I need to do this. I *want* to do this. But there's no operating manual for it." Others told me, "It's not as easy as the traditional stuff like cost cutting or annual planning. I can hire people who do those things they learn in school or during career training. But the purpose stuff is still the Wild West." Stay tuned, as in the pages ahead, we offer up many ideas that you can borrow, adapt, and implement.

- Finally, too many employees at middle and lower levels of organizations do not feel a sense of empowerment on this issue. They feel that purpose is (or is not) handed down from on high and is not something that can be invented on the front lines. As a result, our world loses entire armies of potential difference makers because they've not been empowered to contribute something positive to the world.

Does any of the above sound familiar? We're going to tackle these issues in upcoming chapters. We'll read about dozens of companies who have managed to embrace both purpose and profitability. Perhaps no single group is doing that as well as the newest force at the intersection of cause and capitalism: the B Corps.

The Killer Bs

Traditionally, a company's stated purpose is to aim for maximum return on capital—full stop. In fact, if leaders make a decision that goes against that goal, they can be sued, fired, and stripped of their bonus compensation. But a B Corp represents an entirely new way of incorporating a business, by including written social and/or environmental missions into its founding articles of incorporation.

B Corps can write their charters to clearly state that their aim is not a maximum return but rather a fair one. They send the signal to their investors that if forced to choose between two outcomes, they won't automatically come down on the side that maximizes profits and that they will also evaluate their performance using benchmarks besides profitability.

For example, in addition to traditional financial metrics, a food company might also monitor the ethics of its supply chain and the healthiness of the products it's offering to consumers. A transportation company could commit to having the lowest carbon footprint in its industry. A bottled-water company might pledge to bring clean-water projects to African or Latin American communities with a set percentage of its profits.

A prominent example of this is the popular crowdfunding site Kickstarter. Perry Chen and Yancey Strickler, the company's cofounders, recently announced they would reincorporate as a B Corp. In addition to pursuing profits, they will also include in their corporate charter their mission to "help bring creative projects to life."

"As younger companies come up and think about how they operate and how they want to be structured, maybe they won't be so easily swept up by all the usual choices," Mr. Chen said. "Maybe they'll be thinking long term, thinking about how to look after the things they care about."

This is potentially your future—or perhaps your future competition. Either way, the mere existence of such a path for corporations goes to show how far we've come in rejecting the idea that purpose and profit are mutually exclusive.

Are You Ready for the Revolution?

My genuine hope is that this book will ignite conversations among work teams and leaders at every level of your organization. The conversation will ideally happen with your colleagues at lunch, with friends at the pub, on your alumni group's chat site, and with your family at the dinner table. I want to help provide the insights and the inspiring examples to argue your case for purpose to coworkers within all levels of your organization.

I'm excited to introduce you to dozens of successful businesspeople who are every day proving the case that purpose is not the enemy of profit—that indeed, purpose can help to enhance profitability in both the short and the long term and that it can also make the company more sustainable. These people exist at every level of today's leading organizations, from the CEO to the receptionist. My goal is for the reader to walk away not seeing purpose as a nice-to-have or as something that can be siloed with a single employee or CSR department. I hope that those of you who—like me—have a great deal of faith in capitalism can issue a challenge for capitalism to be more inclusive and impactful.

The world needs solutions to fix all the things that are broken. And I'm convinced that a lot of the solution could lie in a new type of marriage: one that ties the power of capitalism to a larger sense of purpose and meaning.

You Have the Power

So, if you accept the death of this false dichotomy, now what? The question becomes, how can you use your job to change the world? How can you use your current role—not the one you daydream about—to make a difference? How can *you* harness the power of capitalism for societal good?

Can you envision how different your world would be if *work* and *doing good* were no longer at odds but instead lived in blissful and peaceful coexistence? Imagine that dinner-table conversation with your kids when you show them photos of the school your company built in Nepal. Envision how bonded your team will be after spending an afternoon reading with kids in an inner-city school. Think how motivated you will be to sell more product if every SKU sold helps to further a social outcome.

It's time for your potential energy to be turned into kinetic energy. This book will arm you with inspiring stories and how-to examples that you can bring into every meeting and conversation. Together, we'll set you up to express your more altruistic aspirations with others from a place of strength and self-confidence—not only with hard data but also with examples of how companies are using purpose not to diminish profits but to enhance them.

I'm excited to walk you through the steps to convince your company to make a change without freaking anyone out. I'll teach you how to talk to the head in addition to the heart—something I've learned to do in countless boardrooms and convention halls around the world. I'll show you how to get feedback on your idea, build your tribe of coworkers, and convince your superiors that purpose can help your company to achieve greatness. Like Dorothy with her ruby slippers, you've always had the power—you just didn't know it yet.

I've Been to the Mountaintop...

Given my professional trajectory, you might expect me to write a book encouraging you to follow in my footsteps. Ditch the cubicle, and find your cause. That's not what this is.

I'm writing this book so that you *don't* have to follow in my footsteps.

Stay right where you are. Don't climb a mountain in Nepal, don't leave your job, and don't start a charity.

I'm writing this book because it's the book I wish I'd had when I was at Microsoft—a book that would have taught me how to stay in the corporate world *and* at the same time change our society for the better. A book that I could have bought in bulk, taken into meetings, and given to my peers. A book I could have used to help make Microsoft—dominant, cash rich, and seemingly unstoppable at the time—a force for social good in the world.

Today, I no longer believe that the path I took is the only way to change the world. It does not have to be all or nothing.

You don't have to hike high up in the Himalayas to meet your purpose.

Where Do We Go from Here?

The next eight chapters of this book use data, surveys, interviews, and case studies to make the case that a strong sense of purpose can help businesses in myriad ways that directly affect the bottom line. If you made a list of the critical factors needed to make a business successful, many of these would be on your list. We'll show you how purpose can radically increase the chances of success. We're going to knock all eight of them off, one by one, to build our case that purpose is not just for hippie do-gooders but is something that hard-core capitalists should also embrace. Here's a sneak preview of what comes next:

- Connect with prospects and customers in a new way—one based on values, mission, and societal uplift. This wins their hearts and wallets, keeps them coming back, and makes them eager to provide referrals.
- These customers also become your buzz agents. Purpose can inspire them to tell your story via social media. Jaded and overstimulated consumers no longer believe what they hear in paid advertisements, but they do have faith in referrals and recommendations from trusted friends and influencers on social media. Purpose can play a huge role in this rapidly evolving arena.
- Win the war for talent by attracting the best and the brightest, especially those who have a strong desire to make their community and the world a better place.
- Motivate your employee base, inspire them to recruit new talent, and lower attrition among your superstars.
- Unify your business ecosystem, including agencies, vendors, and partners, via a shared sense of mission.
- Attract the best investors—ones who align with you through not just financial goals but also shared values.
- Assure better relationships with government regulators, thereby saving on legal and compliance costs and freeing up scarce leadership bandwidth.

- Stay on the right side of both "citizen regulators," and the increasingly common business-to-business regulators.

This book is my manifesto, a personal appeal from me to you. We need to convince the corporate world that when it makes the critical decision to "embrace and embed" a deeper sense of purpose into its corporate destiny, we will have the ultimate win-win-win.

We will have lives and careers that are full of motivation, meaning, and happiness. We will have better companies that are more motivated and innovative and with higher enterprise value.

And best of all, we will leave a legacy of improved communities and a better world.

I humbly hope that this book can be part of a tipping point in your life and that the moment will arrive when purpose becomes part of your business's DNA and your career. You were not born merely to make money, and neither was your company.

The win-win-win is out there waiting for you to grab it: you help build a great company, and you enjoy a career that has a deeper meaning that motivates you every day, all while simultaneously making the future a better place for our kids to inhabit.

Cause and capitalism can coexist, and it can start with you. Are you ready to help lead this revolution?

A (Blissfully Short) Note on Definitions

Before we dive in, please allow me to quickly clarify what I do (and don't) mean by purpose. It's obviously important to get this right since it's the focus of this book, and many times people have very different perceptions and definitions of the term.

Purpose

Companies that embrace purpose are ones that have chosen to focus on objectives larger than just the traditional financial metrics of success, such as revenues, profits, cash flow, and market share. They've built into their business plan the attainment of social goals that benefit others who live outside the company, not just themselves. And they've done it in a way that is embedded into their company culture and business model.

What Purpose Isn't

There are many misconceptions about purpose, so to be up-front early in the book, it's good to be clear when a company has not truly embraced purpose (or at least not this book's definition of it). Common misconceptions include the following:

- Using purpose as a short-term promotion or one-off initiative (examples could be initiatives such as "day of service" or "week of giving")

- Siloing purpose so that it resides with a single person or department, rather than sharing it widely across the company and baking it into the business model and strategy

- Believing that purpose will be a silver bullet that will solve all your company's problems (You still, of course, need great products, pricing, placement, promotion, and people.)

- Taking a disparate collection of things you're already doing and then wrapping a fancy new slogan around it

- Putting the financial health of your company in jeopardy (The pursuit of both profit and purpose need not involve trade-offs—great companies and leaders find ways to have both.)

2

The Fifth *P*

It's one of the immutable facts of business: you must somehow convince a consumer to exchange his or her hard-earned money for whatever it is that you provide, whether that product has been around for ages (milk! transportation! jewelry!) or is something the consumer has never seen and never knew he or she needed (smartphones! Botox! gluten-free!). It's true that all companies are just metaphorical vendors at an open-air market trying to get people to stop at *their* stalls. But the dizzying reality for the twenty-first-century modern consumer is that the technological revolution has transformed that market into an Escher-like landscape where digital-access providers, vendors, and advertisers are blending in and out of roles, shifting shapes, and disguising their intent. Google, Facebook, Amazon, and Apple are battling to control, if not become, the entire marketplace itself, using the data we provide about ourselves through digital entertainment and communication to create billions of different individual markets, each shaped by our conscious and unconscious choices.

In this four-dimensional world, the modern capitalist needs to connect with the consumer in personal, passionate, idiosyncratic ways to capture his or her attention. If you and I search for a product on Amazon.com, we will each get a uniquely customized product listing that is thousands of items deep. It's even more crowded on Taobao and Tmall, two phenomenally popular shopping sites run by Alibaba, where there are over 7.5 million shops competing for attention. Not products—shops!

The classic four *P*s of marketing—product, price, promotion, and placement—still define the competitive battleground, but they are no longer sufficient. Unless you have first-mover advantage, the odds are good that a rival has already optimized those *P*s long before you and your product arrived. And then what are you left with? What other tools do you have in your arsenal to convincingly say, "Pick me"?

This book proposes a fifth *P*, and luckily for all of us, it is still a largely unclaimed frontier: *purpose*. It's becoming much more common for companies ranging from unknown start-ups to global behemoths to use purpose to win new customers. And when those customers get so excited about the brand's aligned purpose, they become buzz agents, referring their networks to everyone ranging from family to friends to coworkers to social-media followers. No demographic exemplifies the power of the fifth *P* more than millennials.

The M Word

Companies are obsessed with millennials—their habits, their values, their lifestyle choices—and for good reason. Millennials, who were born between 1980 and 2000, are the largest generation in US history.

There are about ninety-two million millennials in the United States, compared to sixty-one million Generation Xers and seventy-seven million baby boomers.

And while you might be tempted to ignore them on public transport, you'd best pay them mind when it comes to engineering a successful business. But this subset of the population is expected to collectively spend more than $200 billion a year starting in 2017 and upward of $10 trillion in their lifetimes.

Millennial customers are clearly an enormous commercial force—with the power to spend and set trends—and it's worth doing away with any residual scorn and work to understand what they want and why they want it.

So, what do they want?

Those Mythical Millennials

There's a long list of boxes you allegedly need to check to win the millennial customer. You're supposed to offer top-notch customer service, access via multiple social-media platforms, and an opportunity to cocreate as well as not take your brand too seriously. But perhaps no tool is more powerful than purpose when it comes to wooing this demographic.

Millennials are given a bad rap for being distracted by technology and self-promotion, but their digital obsession has resulted in an army of young consumers who are more informed about national and world politics than any generation before.

According to a recent Millennial Cause study, six in ten millennials feel personally responsible for making a difference in the world, and more importantly, nearly eight in ten believe that companies have a responsibility to join them in this effort.

When it comes to their purchasing preferences, a Goldman Sachs report found that millennials rank social responsibility higher than any other attribute, including lower price, easy availability, quality, or prestige. "Aspirational consumers," as they're often called, are optimistic about the future and see brands and free-market capitalism as a force for positive change.

That same Goldman Sachs report said that "52% of US consumers claim that they actively seek information about company's CSR records...as more of the millennial generation makes a significant impact on the consumer base, we believe this trend will increase."[1]

Purpose has invaded the capitalistic decision-making process. So, no matter your job—whether you're in sales or PR or product design— you must consider the desires of a constituency that cares about not just the product you want them to buy but the karmic carryover of the transaction.

In 2011, GoDaddy CEO Bob Parsons got major karmic blowback when he posted a four-minute video online of himself shooting and killing an elephant in Zimbabwe. He did nothing to calm the resulting Internet firestorm, telling one *Time* magazine interviewer, "Am I rocked over it? No. Am I sad that I put it up? No. Do I plan to do it again? Yes."

Competitor Namecheap responded by launching a campaign that allowed GoDaddy customers to transfer their .com, .org, and .net domains onto Namecheap's servers for just $4.99 per domain, with the added promise to donate 20 percent from each transfer to Save the Elephants.

The promotion was supposed to last one day but was so popular the company extended it by twenty-four hours and then another twenty-four hours and then another forty-eight hours. It is estimated that over twenty thousand GoDaddy customers decided to migrate their domains to Namecheap.

Customer Pawan Deshpande, the thirty-four-year-old CEO of software start-up Curata, explained his appreciation of this particular cause-marketing campaign: "I thought it was very clever of Namecheap to 'news-jack' all the negative publicity around GoDaddy's CEO and use that to run a marketing campaign to get people to switch over to their service.

"I was already using Namecheap at that point," he says, "but I forwarded their offer to several friends. More importantly, GoDaddy's reputation has been tarnished in my mind, and I have consistently recommended many friends and colleagues to use Namecheap over GoDaddy in light of the GoDaddy CEO's behavior."

Social responsibility makes consumers take notice. According to a newly released College Explorer study from Alloy Media, more than nine in ten of the nation's students say they are less likely to ignore an ad that promotes a brand's partnership with a cause.

And two-thirds of shoppers say simply giving money away isn't enough; they want businesses to integrate social impact directly into their business models.[2]

Shopping for a Better World

The best corporate citizenship initiative goes beyond a short-lived sponsorship; it's about a sustained commitment to a cause that aligns with the core values of the company.

In that spirit, let's talk a little bit about buy-one-give-one campaigns, a model that—on its best days—leverages millennial buying power to help solve social problems.

Since it was founded in 2006, Toms Shoes has given away more than sixty million pairs of shoes in seventy countries and inspired dozens of similar businesses to follow suit. Warby Parker sells and distributes eyeglasses (over three million to date). Roma Boots sells rain boots and donates free pairs to street children and orphans. A product called This

Bar Saves Lives (no attempt to be subtle here!) will donate a packet of life-saving food to a child in need for every granola bar sold.

There's a great deal of debate around the helpfulness of such programs, but you can't deny the appeal they hold for consumers. Not only do millennials opt into them with great frequency, but they *stay* opted in. They return again and again, with a level of product loyalty most companies would kill for.

These programs aren't perfect. But we know from a few studies that they provide tangible benefits that are easy to understand and that meet basic needs. Consumers like the positives—and so do we.

I have a millennial-aged friend who only wears Toms shoes despite the fact that she somewhat jokingly blames them for a recent broken foot. "I was walking down the hallway in my house," says Celia Temkin, "when I turned to my left, lost my balance, and heard a loud *snap*." She says the lack of support from the canvas material allowed her foot to slip off the rubber sole. Six hours later, an ER doctor returned with the news that her foot was badly broken in two places. She was on crutches and then in a boot for six months. "*Six*," she says again, for emphasis. "And perhaps the worst part was the lameness of my story! I wasn't being chased by a lion or saving a baby...I pivoted in a pair of Toms!" Her husband ranted about the shoes ("They did this!") and begged her to toss them out, but Celia believes in the company's buy-one-give-one policy.

In her words: "I know Toms isn't a perfect company, and I understand solving poverty in a sustainable way is more complicated than free shoes, but intent counts for something, and I believe they *mean* to make the world a better place. And as silly as it sounds—it felt selfish to boycott that because my ankles are too weak. Apparently, their mission overrides my common sense. Good for them."

To understand how purpose can help win and thrill customers, you must understand why the buy-one-give-one marketing model is such a winner. "The short answer is that one for one capitalizes on two psychologically important factors," notes Deborah Small, a professor of marketing and psychology at Wharton. "First, people are more sympathetic toward a single identifiable recipient than to unidentified or statistical victims. One-for-one models connect a donor to a specified recipient. Even if we do not know who that person is, our imagination more naturally connects with a single person and heightens responsibility and the motivation to help."

Deborah continues, "Second, people care about making an impact and *perceive* that they are making more of an impact when their actions lead to a concrete and tangible result (e.g., a pair of shoes, glasses). We don't perceive the same impact when our actions are chipping away at a larger problem or moving forward an inch when the end goal is a mile away."

Judging from the number of copycats—and the fact that the private equity giant Bain Capital paid Toms $300 million for a 50 percent stake of the company in 2014—it's clear that the idea of "one for one" has transformed into a profitable business model across various industries, and confirms how important it is to understand the tug of the heart in matters of the cash register.[3]

Come One, Come All

Purpose isn't just for limping millennials, though. It's not like everyone over forty has just disappeared—sucked up into the sky, with their wallets, by the Rapture.

For starters, it's been proven that Gen Xers and baby boomers are starting to communicate and shop like millennials. So, if you can win the millennials as customers, you're likelier to win the other generations as customers—but if you lose millennials, you increase your chances of losing your Gen X and baby boomers as well.

Secondly, it's important to remember that millennials share a lot of characteristics with their baby-boomer predecessors. In generational studies the former are often referred to as "echo boomers," and the original boomers still exert a great deal of influence themselves.

Let me introduce you to one such baby boomer: yours truly.

I've been interacting more than I ever would have expected to with a company that has always seemed big and impersonal to me. It started with a unique offer from them to help me to be a better environmentalist.

My Weekly Purp(ose) Walk

I live in Hong Kong. Specifically, I live on the *island* of Hong Kong and feel blessed to have verdant mountains, gorgeous beaches, and hundreds of kilometers of running and hiking trails within minutes of my front door. Hong Kong is a lot greener than most people realize, because the dazzling skyline is what first draws the eye. One thing that makes it a special place is that hyperactive commercial centers are juxtaposed against tens of thousands of acres of uninhabited (unless you count the wild boars) parkland.

Despite this, Hong Kong is not good at recycling, and this has constantly nagged at my wife and me. That's why I became very interested one day while I was stocking up on coffee capsules at my local Nescafé store when the saleswoman said, "You know, you can save the capsules and bring them back anytime—we recycle them."

I'd wondered about the environmental impact of my coffee consumption, as the move toward single-serve pods can be construed as a bit of an environmental disaster. Because they are made of a combination of aluminum and plastic, they're not able to be recycled by municipal authorities. The majority end up in landfills, where they'll never biodegrade. It has gotten so bad that John Sylvan, the inventor of the K-Cup single-serving coffee pod, America's biggest selling capsule, has foresworn his invention. "I feel bad sometimes that I ever did it," he told one journalist.[1]

So, it was great news that my Nespresso store was encouraging me to stop being part of the problem and to start being part of the solution. As a customer, it makes me happy that this process encourages me to drop by and drop off the used coffee pods for recycling. It gives me a little halo effect on my day. Best of all, the clerks always encourage me to enjoy a coffee on the house at their stand-up espresso bar, often steering me toward new flavors I might not yet have tried.

The entire experience changes how I feel about the brand and myself as a consumer of it—which is what it's about. The issue of purpose is less about millennials or boomers or Generation A, B, or C; it's about the relationship between a company's values and a customer's values.

Purpose, Alignment, and Trust

I'm eager to introduce you to Vicky Tsai and Brad Murray, mainly because they are heroes of mine. When I was debating whether I could find time in my busy life to write this book, their story was one that pushed me across the line. The more time I spent with them, the more convinced I became that this book needed to be written so that stories like theirs could inspire both the believers and the fence-sitters to incorporate purpose into their business models.

Vicky and I originally crossed paths a decade ago while she was leading Starbucks's consumer-products expansion strategy in China.

Her peripatetic life was spent running between Seattle and the mainland. Due to a lack of nonstop flights, she often had layovers at Tokyo's Narita Airport. It was there that she picked up "the most effective skin care products [she'd] ever encountered" from a company she'd never heard of. Skin care was important for Vicky because she'd been suffering from acute dermatitis.

The products, which included a blotting paper to remove excess oil from the skin, worked magically. Upon hearing that the blotting papers had a beautiful history as well, with roots traced back to gold-leaf artisans, she took a big risk. She reached out to the company to ask if they'd be willing to work with her to import this product into the US market.

They rebuffed the offer, but Vicky is one of those people who, once she gets an idea in her head, is not going to let it go. She booked a flight to Japan anyway and let them know she would be in the neighborhood. Intrigued, they agreed.

Are Geisha Even a Real Thing?

During yet another long flight across the Pacific, Vicky prepared her long list of questions. Early in this initial meeting, she was surprised to learn that the products were based on the long-standing beauty rituals that geisha had been following for hundreds of years. The team suggested that if Vicky really wanted to understand the products, she should meet some of the geisha and Kabuki actors who used them every day.

"I thought, are geishas even a real thing?" she now laughs. "Turns out they are! I was soon introduced to my first geisha. She was exquisite. Like living art. Her skin was phenomenally smooth. I asked her if she could tell me about her beauty rituals. She showed me where she gets makeup and how it's produced. I came home to San Francisco with this collection of powders and waxes, and within the month, my skin was transformed. The acute dermatitis that plagued me for years subsided, and my skin was rebalanced, happy, and healthy. I knew I had to recreate these products for others like me."

She was also plotting one more element of her launch strategy—how to instill purpose into the new company's mission. For the last decade, Vicky had been questioning her employment choices, mostly because she did not see how her career was doing anything to make the world a better place. Her first job after graduating from Wellesley was with Merrill Lynch in New York. It was less than two years before her wake-up call arrived with brute force on September 11, 2001.

Prior to September 11, I was very proud of and thankful for my job on Merrill Lynch's bond trading floor because it was considered quite prestigious. At the same time, I knew the job wasn't for me. The minute I stepped on the trading floor, I knew I would die a bit inside every day I stayed there. But I felt I owed it to myself and to the people who gave me the opportunity—my family and mentors—to put my head down, work hard, and do the job well. I thought that after I made a certain amount of money, I would have time to think about who I wanted to be.

[My husband] Eric and I worked in Four World Financial Center, which was connected to the Twin Towers via a land bridge. We were both in the office but separated by twenty floors when the planes hit the towers on September 11, and I couldn't find Eric among all the chaos for a while. I thought I lost my best friend. Experiencing that was a huge wake-up call. Before that day, like most people in their twenties, I had assumed I had the luxury of a long life ahead of me, with plenty of time to figure out what I wanted to do, do good things for other people, and finally be a good person.

September 11 made me realize that if you want to be a good person, be a good person today. If you want to tell your parents you love them, tell them today. And if there is something you want to accomplish in your life, you are responsible for making it happen sooner rather than later, because there is no promise of 'later.' I realized that a lot of things I chased after would be different if I knew that tomorrow would be the end of the road for me, and I decided that I didn't need to wait until a midlife crisis at age forty or fifty to reevaluate my priorities and how to live my life. The trick would be finding work that aligned with all aspects of who I am as a person—my values, my life goals, and my strengths. I didn't want to fake it anymore.

It was because of this vow that Vicky and I were brought together.

Beautiful Faces, Beautiful Futures

As Tatcha, Vicky's geisha-inspired beauty line, began to grow, she recruited a fellow Harvard Business School alumnus, Brad Murray, to join the company as its president.

Vicky and Brad decided that one way they'd differentiate their product was by attaching a social outcome to each purchase. They studied their target audience to determine what would have the greatest resonance and landed on education for young girls. "With most of our customers being women who had benefitted from the opportunities that come with education," Vicky told me, "we wanted to provide them with a way to easily give back and help girls who might not otherwise attend school."

Vicky had seen me speak at Starbucks's annual sales and marketing conference while on my book tour for *Leaving Microsoft to Change the World*, and she had reached out to the partnership team at Room to Read. Together, they developed a strategy under which each Tatcha product sold would result in a donation to Room to Read's long-term Girls' Education Program. Desiring a transparent model, Brad asked, "What does it take to keep a girl in school for a year?" The answer was $250 per year. Bingo! The model was born—for each full-size skin-care purchase, Tatcha would donate the funds to allow one girl to go to school for one day.

They also vowed that this would not be a short-term campaign but rather a permanent part of the business model. "We will do this for every product sold, through every channel, in perpetuity. Many companies do these initiatives during a themed month, which means that eleven months out of twelve, their business is not aligned with any purpose. We vowed to be different."

One girl for one day might sound like a small start, but Vicky and Brad had learned during their days at Harvard Business School how to scale a business. They were not afraid to think big. To inspire their customers, channel partners, and employees with what might be possible, they publicly declared a very bold goal: within five years, they would fund one million days of schooling for young women across the developing world.

Why were they so bullish? Why not just declare, "We'll do the best we can," or shoot for a lower number like ten thousand girl-days? Brad explained that they believed not only in the product but also in the notion that giving back would be a sustainable and differentiating competitive advantage.

"Girls' education was a great fit as we're in the business of making people feel more beautiful, both inside and out," Brad explained. "The idea that every purchase would have an effect on actual girls who wanted an education resonated with our customers, because as women and as mothers, there's a natural inclination to feel guilty when you take care of yourself rather than others."

And being skilled marketers, they devised a memorable and inspiring name for the partnership: Beautiful Faces, Beautiful Futures.

Purpose-Enhancing Profits at Tatcha

So, has it worked? Is there data to prove that the company accomplished more than just giving away profits? Vicky and Brad believe that the campaign has had a huge impact on enterprise value. They don't just believe; they have the data. They outlined for me four key ways the campaign has made Tatcha a more valuable company:

1. The retail channel: Tatcha had to convince its sales channel partners to give its products both breadth and depth of distribution. The company faced formidable barriers. As Brad pointed out to me, "The beauty industry has very low barriers to entry and attracts a lot of players. That is why the industry is full of businesses with less than $5 million in sales. It takes something truly unique to gain real scale, and it's crucial to start from a very solid brand concept."

Their dream was to share the word about their giving program through the retailing giant Sephora, although they were told by some that it would not work. Sephora is the biggest beauty retailer in the United States, with over seven hundred locations. It can make or break a new brand, but according to Vicky, "We were told that Sephora has traditionally not liked focusing on CSR efforts because very few of their brands do it in a substantive way. What happened typically was along the lines of 'Hey, it's Breast Cancer Awareness Month; let's do something where a "portion of the proceeds" goes to a perfectly legitimate organization, and then after a month, we just go back to business as usual.'"

As a result, Sephora would hear a lot of customer backlash, because customers are jaded about marketing and were skeptical of any model that was not clear and transparent. "What is the real impact? Is it genuine? Is it authentic?" Many times the brand placed a "ceiling" on the donation total, so consumers were left wondering whether their purchase had made any difference. But when the woman who heads up skin care at Sephora heard about the Beautiful one-for-one business model—where one Tatcha purchase equals one day of school for a girl—she immediately told Brad and Vicky, "I want to be part of this."

Priya Venkatesh, vice president of skin-care merchandising at Sephora, can testify to the power of purpose in helping Tatcha secure this very important channel partnership: "Tatcha is one of the fastest-growing brands at Sephora because it offers both a compelling brand story and a high-quality, luxurious product line. The brand not only invests in marketing, field, and product development but also in philanthropic efforts that change children's lives through education, like their Beautiful Faces, Beautiful Futures campaign. Our cast and clients are proud to support a brand that gives back to the global community."

2. Customer referrals: According to Vicky, "Skin care is such a loyalty-driven purchase. You work hard to win the customer, so you hate to lose them. Having this built into our business model really helps. I don't think the giving-model piece of it is always the reason people buy the brand in the first place, but I think it's a key reason people *stay* with the brand. Tied to this is the fact that a lot of the growth in the brand has come through word of mouth. A lot of our first-time customers come because of a friend gifting the product to them, and we're more 'giftable' because of the social impact. They share not just the product and its benefits but also the story of the girls whose lives we are changing. People respond to stories, and this is a story people very much enjoy telling. And hearing."

To quantify the impact, Tatcha closely monitors and measures its customers' willingness to promote its brand using a popular measure called the Net Promoter Score (NPS). NPS is a way to measure both customer engagement and the health of a brand, by rating customers in one of three categories: detractors, passive, or promoters. The average company receives a score in the range of twenty to forty-five. Forty-five to sixty is considered excellent, with anything above sixty earning the firm a "superstar" label. Tatcha's NPS is off the charts at eighty!

How have they done it? Vicky explained that "great products alone will not spark this level of passion and advocacy for a brand. We are known in our industry as a values-driven company. Our campaign shows customers that we'll put our money where our mouth is."

3. Social-media buzz: In the beauty industry, word of mouth is often magnified online through social-media influencers. Vicky told me that every time they post the story of a girl scholar in the Room to Read program, "there is this outpouring of love because influencers love the approach. And thankfully for us, it's an outpouring that can be quantified." Tatcha's media agency estimates that to date, mentions by influencers on social-media sites like YouTube, Instagram, and Facebook have exceeded $2.5 million.

4. Traditional media: In late 2016, I ran into Vicky at a party in New York. After too many flights and long hours of working, she had contracted laryngitis, but this did not stop her from running across the room and embracing me in a giant bear hug. "John, we did it!" she whispered in a croaky frog voice. "We hit the goal. We are writing a check next week that will put us over the top on the one-million-girl-days goal!" Our teams immediately began planning outreach to traditional media around this philanthropic accomplishment, which would also include the announcement of a new product to celebrate the goal: the One in a Million Limited Edition Luminous Dewy Skin Mist.

The blurb on Sephora's page read:

> Tatcha's founder, Victoria Tsai, worked with a gold-leaf artisan in Japan to create this limited-edition reusable bottle, commemorating the bestselling treasure that helped the brand fund one million days of education for girls in Asia and Africa, in partnership with Room to Read. The timeless pattern of maple leaves and cherry blossoms represents the unlimited potential for growth for these young women, thanks to the support of this program.

Within two months, the story had been picked up by over forty media outlets, including the Huffington Post, *InStyle*, *Vanity Fair*, and *USA Today*. On the popular style and beauty website Refinery29, it was featured in a story titled, "The One Product Kim Kardashian Swears by for Flawless Makeup." Tatcha's agency estimated the value of this "earned media" at over $1 million.

Purpose as a Competitive Advantage

Tatcha is up against the giants of the industry—from L'Oreal to Clinique to Estée Lauder. These companies spend tens of millions of dollars on advertising everywhere from glossy beauty magazines to duty-free shops at airports. Brad and Vicky believe that their model has helped Tatcha to compete effectively but on a different playing field. I'll let Vicky wrap up the Tatcha story in her own words:

> Our girls'-education commitment really helps us. Our customers are getting inundated with messages from other brands. Beautiful Faces, Beautiful Futures gives us one more method of engagement. Our customer-service reps are all trained to talk about it. It's just one more reason to stay with us, come back and try new products, make repeat

purchases, and that ultimately, in skin care and in any consumer product, is how you build a great business.

The impact of our messages will only grow stronger over time as we reach new milestones and show our customers what an impact they're having simply by purchasing and using our products. It's very powerful, and it cuts through the noise.

Our customers are so happy and inspired when they hear these updates. It's like they're part of a community or a bunch of mothers getting together, and they feel good about being part of something that matters.

Our commitment to girls' education allows us to change the playing field from 'Who has the biggest advertising buy?' or 'Who has hired the hippest model?' to 'Who can most inspire the consumer?' We can cut through a lot of noise because it's differentiated, and it's authentic.

Vicky also offered advice for others seeking to marry cause to capitalism in their own businesses:

Part of the reason we set things up in this way is that it's a time-saving device. The thing I have the least of between being an entrepreneur, a mom, and a wife is free time. So, it helps us to have a system that just makes our philanthropic giving automatic. If Brad and I had to sit down once a quarter and try to figure out how much money we'd made and how much we wanted to give to good causes and then select those causes, it's likely we would not have accomplished much of anything for the world at this point. By having a set plan and formula, it's not something we need precious cycles thinking about. Except for the time, of course, that we spend feeling good about it.

Selling over a million SKUs has done wonders for Tatcha's revenue growth. From 2014 until 2017, its sales increased at a rate of 54 percent per annum, for a total growth of 270 percent. You must tip your hat to them.

The best corporate-cause marketing isn't about a fleeting sponsorship. It's about a long-term commitment to a cause that supports the core values of your business.

A lot of animal-focused businesses also do this well. BarkBox donates 10 percent of all profits to over three thousand shelters and rescues around the United States and Canada. ThunderShirt, Kong, and FroBo all have similar programs that help to give back to the animal community, thus getting them in front of their target audience in a way that helps build trust and loyalty.[5]

Purpose can help a company connect better with its existing customer base; it can also help a company *expand* its customer base, redrawing the borders of its possible profit pool.

I recently committed to switching my home broadband service from the entrenched incumbent to a young upstart. The way this company won me over was 100 percent based on purpose.

"Make Our Hong Kong a Better Place to Live"

When I moved to Hong Kong in 2014, a friend of mine told me, "There's a joke here, and it's not a very funny one, that every day you're a resident, you help to make the richest man in Hong Kong just a little bit richer." That's because Li Ka-shing (net worth: $34 billion) has ownership stakes in companies that are among the few providers of the utilities and services we pay for every day: power, light, and cell-phone service. Adding to the family's collective fortune, his son Richard founded PCCW, which provides home and wireless broadband service and enjoys a market share north of 60 percent.

I've been a PCCW customer for three years. I've had zero problems with their service, I find their technicians to be friendly and competent, and I believe they charge a fair price. But I recently made a decision to move all of my business—voice, mobile, and home wireless—away from the companies that help make the rich even richer. Why? It all started the day I met a guy named NiQ Lai.

I've lectured frequently at the joint-venture executive MBA program run by Kellogg and the Hong Kong University of Science and Technology (HKUST). It was at one of these that I first met a soon-to-graduate NiQ, who shared with me his excitement to have recently joined a company called Hong Kong Broadband Network (HKBN) in the position of CFO. Set up as a direct "David" to the PCCW Goliath, the company's mission statement was to "Make our Hong Kong a better place to live."

The company's original tagline was "Become number one in telco industry," but in 2012, after a change of ownership, the company recognized they needed something more compelling and inspiring. NiQ explained, "We realized that we've been 'making our Hong Kong a better place to live' since we started in 1993, and it's what we wanted us to focus on in the future."

I commented that this was an unusual approach for a technology company, because technology companies usually focus on product attributes. NiQ explained that Hong Kongers have exceptionally strong civic pride in so many aspects of life in the city-state, including strong rule of law, a consistent ranking as one of the world's five most competitive economies, a world-class airport with high-speed rail (twenty-three minutes from the airport to downtown at eighty miles per hour), and lifestyle amenities including five hundred kilometers of hiking trails and clean beaches. HKBN's goal was to connect to that sense of pride by publicly declaring that whether the company made Hong Kong a better place to live would be the litmus test by which it would judge itself and by which the public should also evaluate it.

NiQ, always a bundle of energy, gave me the full scoop at rapid-fire speed:

Our history is that we started offering fiber broadband services in the very dense public-housing segment first. In the early 2000s, we offered broadband at HK$99 per month (US$13) whilst the incumbent was charging HK$500 per month.

We had to make it affordable for the poor to get online. At HK$500 per month, the public-housing segment simply could not afford broadband, which 'caged' them into their poverty even more. I look at access to the Internet like how you and the Room to Read team look at reading—to break the poverty cycle. Economically it made sense for us—we are a for-profit company, and our CAPEX [capital expenditure] per home is lowest in the densest areas of Hong Kong. So, we can afford to charge far less and still be more profitable than the incumbent over time. We were disruptive because we charged a lower cost for fiber broadband than what the incumbent charged for copper broadband. Therefore, we focused on the public-housing segment first. We turned the income pyramid upside down and prioritized those customers who had the least but potentially could gain the most.

I asked NiQ about the "how." The company had a great marketing slogan, but how did they put their ideas into practice? According to NiQ, the company made commitments that include the following:

- **Cost subsidies for the poor:** Because Hong Kong suffers from some of the world's highest income inequality, in the past, before HKBN, the poor were often priced out of having home broadband (which arguably made them poorer). HKBN publicly committed to the policy that the cost of home broadband would never exceed 1 percent of the average household income for Hong Kong families. "You pay just 1 percent (well below global averages) for your family to have world-class broadband, and you have 99 percent left over for everything else."

- **Employee stock ownership:** One of the reasons Hong Kong has such high income inequality is that the old-school capitalists control all the capital. Unlike in Silicon Valley, it's extremely unusual for employees to hold shares in the company. HKBN vowed to be different. NiQ told me, "If our company does well, then that young employee might be able to buy an apartment for his parents or for herself ten or more years earlier than if he or she worked for a company with no equity upside." He admitted when I asked that this meant that he and the other senior managers were sacrificing some potential upside, but he felt strongly that "my family is already doing well enough—why be greedy and then isolate the people I work beside every day?" Every employee who holds equity in HKBN has one word in common on his or her business card: *co-owner*. The hope is that while employee retention will be strong, the company will also see some of those trained at HKBN become entrepreneurs starting similar values-driven businesses.

I was immediately sold. Issues like income inequality can feel overwhelming, but here was a concrete step I could take as a consumer to support a vision and values that matched my own. Because I had never heard anything even remotely this mission-driven from PCCW, I made the commitment to switch. I've also started my own campaign to convince the residents of the other 120 apartments in my building to also migrate to HKBN. And the minute HKBN announced its entry into the mobile market, I was first in line to give it even more of my business.

HKBN is one of my favorite examples of how a company does not even need a CSR department when its business model clearly links cause to capitalism in a way that's understood across the entire company. And it's clearly working, as they've now captured a home broadband market share of 40 percent. Seven thousand miles east of Hong Kong, in the Bay Area of Northern California, is another inspiring example that you also may not have heard of.

Hungry for Change

You may have never heard of Kristin Richmond and Kirsten Tobey, but they serve more lunches to hungry diners than all but the largest of restaurant groups. That's 300,000 lunches per day, 1.5 million lunches per week, in over one thousand locations. And those numbers are growing so rapidly that they'll be obsolete soon after this book goes to print. Their customers dine with them in thirty cities spread across the United States,⁶ in places ranging from New Orleans to New Jersey and from Denver to Oakland. And believe it or not, the clear majority of their customers dine with them *every single day of the week*.

Do these two entrepreneurs run a trendy restaurant group that you've never heard of? Do they have some hot new show on the Food Network that you've somehow overlooked? Neither of the above! Chances are you've not heard of them because you're not their target demographic. Sorry to spoil your day, but basically— you're too old for them!

Richmond and Tobey were classmates at Berkeley's Haas School of Business in 2006 when they met in a marketing class. One of their assignments involved pitching business ideas on how to make healthy food more accessible to young people—and not just those who come from families who can afford to shop at Whole Foods. Together, they hit on a radical idea. They'd reinvent one of the most unhealthy meals in America: the school lunch!

If you've never had the "pleasure" of eating school lunch in an American public school, you may not be aware that it's less than ideal—or in the words of the *Economist*, "reheated, void of nutrition, and largely unappetizing." Most lunches "are still made rather like airline food. Meals are put together in large processing centers, packaged, sometimes frozen, and then shipped across the country. When they arrive, the lunches are simply reheated. This is certainly cheap, but [it] does nothing for taste, freshness or nutrition."⁷

As if that's not bad enough, the quality of the average school lunch has an uncontrollable factor that makes its quality even worse. Since many children in America come from poor families who qualify for free or subsidized school lunch, the US Department of Agriculture will offer tons of surplus food—cheese, corn syrup, white flour, you name it—to the providers of school lunches. So, the type and quality of the ingredients is often not decided based upon what is best and healthiest for the consumer.

In other words, your child's diet—during a very important time of day when his or her young brain and body need to be fortified for the second half of the school day—can be seriously suboptimal. Is there a way that purpose-driven businesses can help us do better?

You Say You Want a Revolution?

Richmond and Tobey were passionate about changing this broken system. Prior to entering Haas, both had worked in education, in locations ranging from Kenya to Latin America to the United States. Richmond reported that they had both seen "incredible differences—in kids in the classroom and outside of the classroom—between those who were well nourished and those who were not. We both felt like access to healthy, delicious, affordable food was absolutely critical to set students up for success."[8]

With the motivation that comes from a strong sense of purpose, the two "moms on a mission" launched Revolution Foods. Their goal: to provide students with healthy, affordable, and all-natural school lunches. They would avoid junk-food staples such as high-fructose corn syrup and trans fats. Their food would be hormone- and antibiotic-free, and whenever possible, organic. They'd avoid deep-fat frying. And they'd test their products prior to launch on the students themselves.

It was not destined to be easy. Nobody is more likely to tell you that your food sucks than an opinionated and "hangry" eight-year-old (you can imagine the test subjects using terms like *icky* and *blech*). The team recalls being asked by Washington, DC, schools to reinvent a popular favorite: the chicken wing! It took over one thousand attempts—complete with focus groups and tastings—to create a child-approved baked chicken wing infused with a spicy sauce.

They also had to work within schools' existing budgets. It's one thing to create a healthy meal at home when you're swiping your credit card to buy kale and organic salmon at the local co-op. But how do you do it when the local school district has a budget of three dollars per meal?

Starting with the Oakland School District, the cofounders offered their best pitch: "What if we could deliver a meal that your students loved, at the same price, but that was nutritious and sustainable and helped students to have more energy and a higher ability to concentrate during the latter half of the school day?

The pitch was difficult for administrators, teachers, and parents to resist. As a result, the company grew quickly. Starting with just six employees in Oakland in 2006, they were soon opening kitchens to serve school districts in Colorado, Louisiana, New Jersey, and Texas. Today, they have over seventeen hundred employees and have expanded into supermarkets with healthy retail options ranging from granola to "superfood lunch bundles" that include chickpeas, dark-chocolate raisins, corn and flax chips, and almonds.

Employees and investors love that more than 75 percent of the company's school meals go to low-income students.[9] They are not just serving elite students but making it a true "revolution" by helping lower-income students to eat well.

As the *Economist* wrote: "Everyone from Michelle Obama to Jamie Oliver is trying to improve children's diets, but doing so has proved difficult. It is, then, particularly interesting that a solution is emerging from the private sector."[10]

Richmond, one of those two moms on a mission, loves the

feedback the company receives. "I'll never forget when we launched in New Orleans for the first time and had teachers writing in saying, 'My kids are now well nourished. My students are more engaged; I'm seeing they're more focused in class.'"

Healthy Food, Healthy Profits

Revolution is a great example of a company that is doing well by doing good and creating a strong relationship with its customers. By showing every day and with every meal that they care about helping kids lead healthier lives, it's developing a tight bond with parents and with school administrators, who are of course the ultimate decision makers on who gets to serve lunch to their kids.

Even old-line pioneering organic-food company WhiteWave Foods discovered in 2017 that sourcing and selling healthy, high-quality, sustainably sourced food can lead to profits and a fruitful financial legacy, when it sold the business for $10 billion to Danone, the French food group. WhiteWave had been spun out of Dean Foods, an old-school company, with a goal to be "purpose-driven, values-based builders, doers, and believers who are passionate about making better food for a better world and a better future." Its product portfolio included Silk soy milk, Wallaby organic yogurt, Earthbound Farm salad greens, and Horizon Organic dairy products—all major brands in the healthy food space.

By the 1980s, the health-food sector was characterized by smaller companies and nontraditional entrepreneurs who were passionate about helping people to have healthier diets and live longer lives and at the same time being kinder to both animals and the planet. They then connected their customers to those lofty goals, in a conversation that was less about profit and more about purpose. Now some of those pioneers are retiring with a very comfortable nest egg because investors like Danone realized that health foods were one of the only categories where they could find premium prices, high margins, and top-line revenue growth.

CVS and Cigarettes

If most of you associate health-food products with the Purpose Inc. economy, probably few would expect to see drugstore giant CVS planting its flag in this territory. But that happened when the seventy-seven-hundred-store category killer realized it had a huge problem. CVS had to decide whether to continue to carry a product known to be detrimental to its customers' health.

This was not a decision to be made lightly—especially since cigarette sales resulted in over $2 billion of annual revenue. Cigarettes also carry high profit margins, and since the product is completely addictive, it leads to repeat store visits.

But the company was undertaking a major transition; they no longer wanted their customers to think of them as the convenient corner drugstore but as a fully integrated health-care company. While most shoppers see CVS as a place to pick up eye drops, ChapStick, and Hallmark cards, far fewer know CVS is the country's biggest operator of health clinics. The company had changed its name to CVS Health and was expanding its MinuteClinic walk-in health centers. The company now manages pharmacy benefits for sixty-five million customers, and has nine hundred walk-in medical clinics. CVS made $177 billion in revenue in 2016, making CVS one of America's biggest health-care companies.

What signal did it send to customers if they were encouraged to buy a pack of Marlboro Reds on the way to the clinic to visit with a doctor?

The firm's leadership, despite knowing that the decision would likely have an immediate effect on revenues, made their momentous decision to give up $2 billion in revenue. They declared in a press release that "ending the sale of cigarettes and tobacco products at CVS Pharmacy is simply the right thing to do for the good of our customers and our company. The sale of tobacco products is inconsistent with our purpose—helping people on their path to better health."

Other smaller independent chains had already decided to stop selling tobacco, but CVS was the first large chain to do so. One internal change agent was the firm's chief medical officer, Troyen A. Brennan, who explained the strategy: "We know that more than two-thirds of smokers want to quit—and that half of smokers try to quit each year. We also know that cigarette purchases are often spontaneous. And so we reasoned that removing a convenient location to buy cigarettes could decrease overall tobacco use."[11]

How Do We Find an Extra $2 Billion?

As we've said, it's not enough to simply "do the purpose thing" and be self-satisfied. Purpose must be aligned with business objectives— and vice versa—or else everything fails. No company equals no money equals no mission.

The leadership team at CVS challenged itself to not just lose the revenue but to instead find new sources to replace it. The firm's employees were enlisted in a purpose-driven quest to not only help their customers live healthier lives but to also find replacement revenue. The space that had been used for cigarettes was converted to sell higher-margin beauty and food products. The stores marketed nicotine patches and saw a 45 percent increase in sales.[12] The average number of visits to its MinuteClinics for smoking-cessation counseling nearly doubled in the first year after the ban.[13] CVS pharmacists filled nearly six hundred thousand nicotine-replacement-therapy prescriptions.[14] They also pursued new business opportunities brought on by the Affordable Care Act and acquired over sixteen hundred pharmacies from Target, which they would run as a store within a store, branded as CVS Pharmacy.

Within a year, despite the huge revenue gap from lost cigarette sales, the company reported that annual revenue had increased—

proving once again that purpose does not have to be the enemy of profit. And while it may be intangible, one can only imagine how much better it feels to not be aiding and abetting in the poor health and even deaths of your loyal customers.

When Norman de Greve joined CVS Health as chief marketing officer in 2015, the company's plans to phase out tobacco were already rolling. That, of course, was part of the reason he wanted to join. "When I was seven years old, lung cancer took my father's life and took him from me. So, the decision to join CVS Health wasn't just business; it was also very personal."

A year later, to mark the one-year anniversary, the company released the results of a study that examined the impact of its decision to exit tobacco on public health. It showed the following:

- Since the company stopped selling tobacco, there had been an additional 1 percent reduction in cigarette-pack sales across all retailers in states where CVS Pharmacy had a 15 percent or greater share of the retail pharmacy market, compared to states with no CVS Pharmacy stores.
- Over the same eight-month period, the average smoker in those states purchased five fewer cigarette packs, and in total, approximately 95 million fewer packs were sold.
- A 4 percent increase in nicotine-patch purchases in those same states during the period immediately following the end of tobacco sales, indicated that there was also a positive effect on attempts to quit smoking.

Additionally, five hundred thousand consumers visited the section of the company's site devoted to quitting smoking—which remarkably enough is the same number of Americans who die early each year due to smoking. The pivot also scored one hundred million media impressions for CVS Health and overhauled the way people saw the brand. In before-and-after tracking of its corporate image, CVS measured whether influencers thought of the firm as "a leader in helping people improve overall health" as a result of its decision to exit tobacco. CVS Health's research showed a 40 percent lift in brand image.

Larry Merlo, president and CEO of CVS Health, explained to me: "Without question, going tobacco-free was a bold decision for our company and the right decision for our brand, our business, and for the health of the country. First, I think the decision helped to validate our role in the health-care marketplace. If we wanted CVS Health to be credibly viewed as a setting where health care is delivered, then the sale of tobacco had no place in our business model.

"Second, the fact that companies and consumers are now seeing us as a convenient and affordable point of access for quality care creates longer-term growth opportunities for our business. Most importantly, our decision to exit tobacco has made a positive impact on public health. I think a decade from now, we'll look back on our exit from tobacco as a truly seminal moment in our company's history, evolution, and continued success."

"e for Education"

A final example of a company using purpose to connect with customers is the global financial giant Citibank. In 2013, the bank's foreign exchange division was making an all-out push to win business for its new Velocity electronic-trading platform. The bank had two goals: to win business away from rival banks, and to move their own customers away from more expensive manual transactions. In a brainstorm meeting, a group of front-line employees and division management came up with an idea – incent customers by promising them that every Velocity trade during a fixed period of time (typically 4-6 weeks) would generate a contribution to education causes.

I learned from an interview with Caryn Freiberger, a VP on the Foreign Exchange Institutional Sales Desk, that education was chosen because of the bank's "conviction that an investment in education is a global force multiplier. We wanted a catalyst to further activate Citi's mission of enabling progress beyond our conventional business goals." A globally-diverse group of seven education initiatives were selected, including Civic Builders, EMpower, Room to Read, Teach First and Uncommon Schools. Clients were advised that each million dollars traded would generate a dollar of new money for these organizations, and then encouraged with the promise that "the more you trade, the more we donate."

One dollar out of a million may sound small, but Caryn told me that trades in excess of a billion dollars were not uncommon and could happen many times per trading day. "Trust me", I was told, "this is going to work out very well for you." My thoughts quickly turned to Tatcha, where I'd learned to focus less on the contribution per transaction, and more on the possible scale of those transactions.

Caryn's prediction turned out to be accurate. Customer enthusiasm and uptake were higher than anticipated, tied partly to having chosen a cause that was "a strong shared value" with many clients. This also led to great word of mouth and a high level of referrals. The result: in the first year, Citi gave the seven education organizations "significantly more than initially budgeted." To Caryn and the team, this was good news – "this meant we reached more children, while having more clients trading on Citi Velocity than anyone had expected. It's exactly the type of high quality problem we like to have."

The program has now run for five years, and has "created an additional common bond. Through purpose we've deepened the relationship between our sales teams and our clients." Over $20 million has been raised for the bank's education portfolio.

It was not just customers who were excited. Since a later chapter focuses on the ability of purpose to motivate employees, let's let Caryn have the last words:

"For me, one of the most exciting outcomes is the legacy of improving communities in many of the countries where Citi has a local presence. Our global footprint is a core strength of Citi's business and culture. The campaign demonstrated the power of our footprint in a tangible way. Pictures of teammates in London hosting children on trading floors and colleagues in Singapore conducting practice interviews with teenagers we support are incredible reminders of our impact. Not only am I filled with pride, but I also believe my global teammates share my excitement about the opportunities our business is creating."

Closing Thoughts

As motivational speaker and marketing consultant Simon Sinek said in a popular TED Talk ("Start with Why"): "People don't buy what you do; they buy why you do it. Customers want to connect to the story behind the brand. Customers want to know about your purpose in life, why you get out of bed in the morning, and why your organization exists."

The integration of purpose didn't necessarily come from some great corporate "aha moment." It emerged in response to consumers beginning to make real purchasing decisions based on the values of a company, not just the products themselves. They still care about the traditional four Ps of product, price, promotion, and placement. But in a world overrun with consumer choices, the fifth P can gain consumers' increasingly fragmented attention, act as a tie breaker between competing products, and (as we will see in the next chapter) generate buzz on social media.

Postscript

The Tatcha campaign for girls' education had an unexpected effect on Vicky Tsai. During a trip to Cambodia to meet some of the girl scholars benefitting from Tatcha's support, Vicky was not the only one touched by the girls' stories of strength and resilience. Her four-year-old daughter, Alea, made many new friends, and on the long flight back to San Francisco, she chattered constantly about how unfair it is that so many girls don't get to go to school and how excited she was to have new friends who were finally able to go to school every day.

Two days after arriving home, she showed up at the dinner table and introduced her parents to a special guest. Mr. Elephant, her pachyderm equivalent of a piggy bank, was hoisted onto the dining-room table. Alea had decided that he'd be converted into an agent for change. From that moment forward, all money deposited with him would be donated to help more girls go to school. She then hit her parents up for the first twenty-dollar contribution.

She did not stop there. For her birthday parties, she asked that in lieu of gifts, contributions be made to help more girls in Cambodia. She even ran a lemonade stand and discovered, like her mother, how motivated customers would be to buy her product.

As Vicky told me the story, her eyes filled with both tears and maternal pride. "She's now so into helping the cause, and by constantly lobbying us, she often liberates ten- and twenty-dollar bills from our wallets. And really, how can we resist? She's most excited about going back and knowing that just as her mother's company has put girls in school, so have she and her elephant bank. Though she's still very young, this has already been life changing for her."

3

Purpose and Social Media

Another benefit that accrues to companies whose customers and prospects appreciate that they've embraced purpose: they're likely to enjoy a positive buzz on social media. We humans love to tell stories to each other, and various social-media sites have become the new watercooler—a global one where opinions are instantly shared across borders. We talk about what we love and what we hate, and our opinions are then amplified by others who comment, like, and share.

So, if your company is doing things that are socially useful, it's likely that people are talking about it. And that's potentially huge, because so many companies are scrambling to figure out how to optimize their strategy for this relatively new phenomenon, but very few have managed to do so. Most of them won't admit that—they'll claim to have a social-media strategy that is "robust" (they know this because they do "competitive benchmarking"), "cross platform," and optimized for mobile ("mobile first!"). They likely use "geo tagging," are hosted "in the cloud," and are best in class at both "big data" and "machine learning."

Much of this is just a smoke screen, gorillas throwing dust in the air. I think it would be OK to just admit that we've not yet figured it all out, because there are so many reasons that it's not an easy slam dunk:

- It's all very new. The major players in social media didn't even exist fifteen years ago.
- It's rapidly evolving, with a constant stream of new players, rising stars, fizzlers (anyone remember Myspace?), and niche players.
- There are multiple players (Pinterest, WeChat, Signal, Facebook, Twitter, Snapchat, LinkedIn, WhatsApp, Weibo, Google Plus—the list goes on and on), and there are no global standards—if you're on WeChat, almost nobody in Brazil cares. If you're not on it, almost all of China will find you irrelevant. But both Twitter and Facebook are banned in China, and if you're on Pinterest, you're not going to be talking to many men.

If nature abhors a vacuum, agencies and consultants love 'em! A whole new career lock-in is now possible for those who can convince company leaders (many of whose first technology experience was *Pong* rather than sexting disappearing videos) that they've got this whole social-media thing figured out. They engage in a constant cacophony I refer to as "B-3": Buzzword Bullshit Bingo.

Mashable said it best: "Many people overuse buzzwords just to try to sound smart, when in fact they have no idea what's going on."[15]

Here's one thing we do know: when companies do good things, people tend to talk about it, just as we witnessed with Tatcha. And if your company does bad things, don't be surprised when people talk about it even more (stay tuned for a doozy of an example). It's basic stimulus response. Humans are social creatures, and we like to share. It's not only customers who opine on social media—so will employees, journalists, and both government and citizen regulators. While your company can't control the "output," you can control the raw material with which the public has to work.

New York Times business writer Farhad Manjoo opined that every leader must do more of that than he or she probably imagines, because brands are suddenly more vulnerable to consumer sentiment than they've ever been in the past:

It all comes down to one thing: social media is the new TV. In the era when television shaped mainstream consumer sentiment, companies enjoyed the enormous power to alter their image through advertising. Then came the Internet, which didn't kill advertising but did dilute its power. Brands now have little say over how their messages get chewed up through our social feeds.[16]

This new landscape can be either a weakness or a strength for companies. Just as bad news and negative opinions spread like wildfire, the same is also true for positive sentiments. A personal example: one December I was delighted to learn upon boarding a six-hour cross-country Virgin America flight that "the Wi-Fi is complimentary this month—Seasons Greetings from our friends at Google"; I immediately Tweeted a shout-out to both brands to my 380,000 followers.

Social-media reactions to company behavior are often way beyond what the marketing and communications teams could have ever come close to foreseeing. Allow me to share with you two examples—one of a company that got it oh so wrong, and one that not only nailed it but continues to do so on an annual basis.

"It Just Felt Nefarious"

On July 11, 2016, a little-known Brooklyn actress named Mellini Kantayya posted an online petition that would bring a major pharmaceutical company to its knees and its CEO into the hot seat nobody wants to be in: testifying before the US Congress after being accused of price gouging.

The focus of Kantayya's petition was the pharmaceutical company Mylan. Mylan distributes a lifesaving product that many families depend on: the EpiPen. The product is used to treat severe allergic reactions (technically, the appropriately scary-sounding anaphylactic shock) by injecting an automatic dosage of epinephrine into the patient. The causes of anaphylactic shock can range from insect bites to bee-stings to peanut allergies. Most cases are sudden onset, and the symptoms (which include a swelling of the throat and tongue, vomiting, and low blood pressure) can kill a patient who is not treated within minutes.

Mylan provides a widely distributed product that tackles these problems and saves lives—often the lives of adorable little kids! So, what's not to love?

In a word: the price. In four words: the constantly rising price. Under the leadership of CEO Heather Bresch, Mylan had been steadily raising EpiPen prices—first by 10 percent, with the adjustments happening twice a year, and then later by 15 percent. Given the power of compounding, the pricing ultimately soared by over 500 percent during the last decade. Any difficulties families had purchasing the product at such a high price were exacerbated by two factors: many families keep multiple EpiPens stored in numerous locations—school, home, grandparents—so that they are near at hand for any emergency, and because the medicine has a short shelf life, the pens must be replaced frequently—as often as once a year.

These factors contributed to the breaking point for Mellini Kantayya. One day she received an email from a friend in Connecticut whose daughter had severe food allergies. The friend complained that she had been presented with a bill for $600 for the purchase of two EpiPens. The product costs approximately twenty dollars to manufacture, so the markup to the ultimate consumer was 1,500 percent.

"It just felt nefarious," Ms. Kantayya told the *New York Times*. She was familiar with the product, as her husband had allergic conditions, but in her case, the family's health insurance covered the cost. But this did not stop her from protesting. "Just because we're not paying for it, we're still paying for it in terms of social cost." She then thought, "Why don't I do a petition, and maybe something will be done about this."[17]

She drafted a petition titled "Stop the EpiPen Price Gouging" and posted it to Petition2Congress.com, a service that aggregates signatures and delivers them to the relevant leaders in government. She then sent the link to 836 friends on Facebook, with the concise comment, "Stupid pharmaceutical company."

What happened next shows the power of social media to help mobilize and influence consumers. In the span of forty-five days, Ms. Kantayya's petition went from a few dozen signatures to more than eighty thousand, all of whom helped to send more than 121,000 letters to Congress. One mother, the second to sign the petition, told the *New York Times*, "It's just morally so wrong. I have a lot of friends with children with allergies, so we all are pretty adamant about this kind of stuff and support each other."

Perhaps inevitably, an #EpiGate hashtag was created and helped to further spread the word, resulting in Tweets like these:

- "If Mylan is the firefighter than you have to pay $600+ to break the glass to use the fire extinguisher. #epigate."
- "What evil, evil people. Don't #foodallergy families have enough problems?"

For social-media campaigns to be successful, it's not necessary to get millions of likes or retweets. Sometimes all you need is for the right people to be paying attention. This campaign began to gain serious momentum when two things happened. First, major media caught wind of the story, which soon had coverage in outlets including CNN, MSNBC, the *New York Times*, and the *Washington Post*. Politicians also joined in the chorus, with both Democratic presidential contenders on the campaign trail—Hilary Clinton and Bernie Sanders—challenging and criticizing Mylan on their social-media feeds. Soon, an invitation to come into the US Congress for a little chat arrived on CEO Bresch's desk.

Bresch did not help herself as she denied responsibility and tried to deflect it to others. *Time* magazine, in a post titled "Why the EpiPen Price Scandal Sums Up Everything We Hate about Big Business & Politics," reported that "rather than own up to the idea that it was absurd and unfair to jack up EpiPen prices by 600%...Bresch's initial reaction to criticism over the matter was to blame Obamacare and the rise of high-deductible health insurance plans. The fault lies in 'a broken system,' she said while failing to mention that this system also allowed her pay to increase 700%."

While many families were struggling to keep up with the constantly increasing EpiPen prices, Bresch had been enjoying total 2015 compensation of $25 million.[18] Amazingly, she was not even the highest-paid person at Mylan; the board chairman, Robert Coury, had pulled down nearly four times that number—a whopping $97 million. The narrative was all too easy to construct: greedy executives who were willing to screw over customers living from paycheck to paycheck, even if it put children's lives at risk, all in pursuit of feathering their already well-upholstered nests. This also allowed both mainstream-media and social-media critics to point out the hypocrisy of the company's vow to "Do what's right, not what's easy" and the core values listed on its website, such as "We challenge every member of every team to challenge the status quo."

Status Quo, Prepare to be Challenged

Bresch's testimony before Congress opened an entire Pandora's box that made the remainder of 2016 and 2017 a living hell for the company's management. Observant watchdogs in the federal government decided to review whether Medicaid had suffered from price gouging by Mylan, and...surprise—it had! The extent was so large that Mylan quickly settled with the attorney general's office with a $465 million payment. Management, continuing to use only the finest of weasel words, claimed that the "terms of the settlement do not provide for any finding of wrongdoing on the part of Mylan Inc. or any of its affiliated entities or personnel."[19]

The large cost of the settlement caused Mylan to publicly announce a lower forecast for Q3 2016 earnings. This led to a further decline in their already-tanking share price. From a price of $48.66 just before the first petition, the stock fell as low as $35 by mid-November, a 28 percent decrease. This dramatic decrease in market capitalization—over $5 billion—resulted in shareholders filing a lawsuit against the management team and the board. Shareholders also filed motions to decrease executive compensation and to replace the entire slate of board members.

Bresch suffered further embarrassment when it was revealed that she had claimed to have earned an MBA degree despite having completed only half the required classroom work and not having received a diploma.[20]

Finally (and by this point of the story, even I'm beginning to feel a bit sorry for it), the company was also widely excoriated for requiring schools that received EpiPens to sign noncompete agreements, effectively promising not to buy equivalent products from any current or future producer. "Do what's right" indeed.

Meanwhile, as Mylan continued to shoot itself in the foot, companies that were more purpose driven were moving to provide a better solution to families. Responding to the EpiPen controversy, pharmacy giant CVS began working with Impax, the manufacturer of a generic version of epinephrine, to bring out a low-cost version of their product at significant scale. In contrast to the $600 price tag for two of Mylan's EpiPens, the price for the same offering from CVS and Impax would be about one-sixth, or $109.

Many mommy bloggers were only too happy to point out that CVS Pharmacy was run by Helena Foulkes, a mother of four children. Robyn O'Brien, a former food-industry analyst, author, and mother of four, wrote, "Mylan's monopoly has put too many lives at risk. They've priced consumers out of securing the devices needed to protect their loved ones. CVS stepped in to help."[21]

At the time of this writing, exactly one year after Mellini Kantayya launched her "mouse that roared" petition, Mylan's troubles have not gone away. A group of state attorneys general claims that the $465 million penalty was not even close to the amount Mylan cheated out of governments, and it is seeking a $1.3 billion settlement. At a time of very buoyant stock markets, Mylan's shares remain tied to a lead balloon—20 percent below its closing price the day before the petition was filed and nearly 50 percent beneath its three-year high.

Mylan is a classic case study in how companies can very quickly lose control of the narrative in the age of ubiquitous social media. Thankfully, for those of us who are *converts* to purpose-driven companies, there are also positive examples. So, put on your best Christmas-themed sweater, grab a cup of hot cocoa (don't forget the marshmallows), and join me on a little trip to north of the snowy Canadian border.

WestJet's Christmas Miracle

While Heather Bresch and Robert Coury may have deserved to get coal in their stockings, an upstart Canadian airline pulled off a Christmas miracle that is at the opposite end of the social-media spectrum. WestJet is the Calgary-based carrier that models itself on Southwest— think low fares, friendly service, and staff who treat you like they're happy you're on board. Some of those employees cooked up a little surprise in 2013.

As Calgary-bound passengers in Toronto and Hamilton got to their boarding gates one Saturday morning, a virtual video Santa encouraged them to scan their boarding passes. To the surprise and delight of the passengers, the screen immediately came to life, and they "went live" with the North Pole. "Ho ho ho! Is that you, Conner?" Santa asked as the eight-year-old boy's eyes lit up and expanded to the size of saucers. "What do you want for Christmas? A choo-choo train? Ho ho ho! Do you like Thomas?" Dozens of passengers were soon lining up, eager to connect with Santa, requesting everything from "new socks and underwear" to an Android tablet to a wide-screen television.

Unbeknownst to the 250 passengers, as the two flights took off, more than 150 WestJet employees in their destination city of Calgary were scrambling to make those Christmas dreams come true. The employees had just under four hours to take their shopping lists to the mall, make hundreds of purchases, drive to the airport, unload, and begin the process of wrapping and tagging each gift.

Upon arrival at their baggage carousel, passengers smiled as snowflakes fell from the ceiling and WestJet employees offered up hot chocolate and cookies. Soon, the *nant-nant-nant* noise announced that the bags were arriving. But not quite yet. First came several hundred presents, all perfectly wrapped, bearing large tags reading "To Connor, from Santa" and "To Kevin, from Santa." The faces of parents lit up with wide smiles as their kids jumped up and down, pointing at the gifts and then joining the gleeful search for a box with their name on it. "No way!" shouted the boy as he unwrapped the Android tablet he'd asked for just four hours earlier. There were tears of joy and then loud cheers as "Santa" himself entered the baggage-claim area. "Ho, ho, ho! Merry Christmas!" he chortled as he was greeted with high fives and warm hugs.

The WestJet crew even managed to get the fifty-inch TV delivered to the oversize delivery area. (One has to wonder if the guy who asked for socks and underwear looked on while regretting not thinking bigger. "Wait, wait, did I say socks? What I meant to say was…stocks! Lots of stocks!")

The Christmas-miracle idea originated with a group of WestJet employees. The firm's sponsorship lead, Greg Plata, explained that "In early August, we sat down with our friends at Studio M [their agency] and started brainstorming what 'giving' looked like at its best. We wanted to do something big, exciting, and fresh."

Mission accomplished, Mr. Plata! The Christmas miracle video, featuring scenes shot in all three airports, quickly went viral. The "WestJet Christmas miracle" was the number-one trending topic globally the day after launch, WestJet generated more than one billion Twitter impressions in just one month, and more than 235 countries viewed the video, reaching more than thirty-five million views in a month.

And people did not just watch, they commented—thousands of times on social media platforms ranging from Twitter to Facebook:

- "You made my mascara run."
- "This is why I fly with you guys."
- "I've watched it three times now and still crying with each viewing!"
- "This shows that in a world where few big companies seem to care, you're setting an example they should follow."
- "I've never heard of you, WestJet, but after seeing this video I will fly you whenever possible!"

Major media also picked up on the story, with more than sixteen hundred stories in television news, magazines, and newspapers. This created a positive feedback loop—more media led to more views, with more media paying attention as the viewership numbers went higher and higher. Ultimately the story earned more than 328 million media impressions from around the world. Most importantly, WestJet's website traffic was up 100 percent from the year before, bookings were up 77 percent, and revenue was up 86 percent!

More Miracles

Due to the program's popularity with both customers and staff, the Christmas miracle became an annual event. In 2014, a sleigh popped up in a poor village in the Dominican Republic, a destination the airline had recently added. A live video feed to a surprisingly fluent-in-Spanish Santa (*"Feliz Navidad, amigos y amigas!"*) allowed both young and old to make their Christmas wish ("I'm a motorcycle taxi driver, but my engine is broken. And to support my children, I wish I would be granted a new engine.") Señor Santa did not let anyone down, and at the delivery party, hundreds of children were even able to play in the (artificial) snow for the first time in their lives.

In 2015, WestJet employees were challenged to create twelve thousand "minimiracles" over the course of twenty-four hours—that's one act of kindness for every employee. Employees were soon on the streets of New York giving warm blankets to the homeless, picking up the tab for tea drinkers and bar patrons in London, and surprising three children who had recently lost their father to cancer with a spontaneous trip to Disney World. My personal favorite miracle involved a disabled veteran who had served with the Canadian Army in Afghanistan. As he was reunited with his family, they were told that in honor of his service and to make the reunion more special, the entire family was being given round-trip flights to Hawaii.

Each year, the social-media buzz helped to reinforce multiple company objectives, including recruiting ("All I want for Christmas is a JOB AT WESTJET!!! Your team is fabulous, and I would love to be a part of it")[22] and employee motivation ("Having the opportunity to put smiles on people's faces while doing good deeds in communities around the WestJet world defines who we are as a company and reflects our caring corporate culture. It's a testament to how we treat our guests who fly with us.")[23]

Purpose Reflects Values

It might be tempting to question whether the firm did this just to gain attention. After all, there were lots of cameras capturing all the action. I asked a Canadian friend who flies WestJet about this, and she replied that her perception was that the campaign simply reflected the firm's core values—which I promptly looked up, learning that they include "positive and passionate in everything we do," "appreciative of our people and guests," "fun, friendly, and caring," and "honest, open, and keep our commitments."

According to Richard Bartrem, the firm's vice president of marketing and communications, "For WestJet's second Christmas Miracle video, we wanted to turn our holiday campaign into a tradition by doing something that's never been done before. We were inspired by the notion of real-time giving and wanted to surprise our guests with meaningful, personalized gifts when they least expected them. Being able to show our guests how much we care with gift-giving, a tried and true holiday tradition, also resonated with WestJetters as much as our guests."

WestJet demonstrates again how purpose can benefit a company when it's not something that is siloed in a CSR department. They have made the tradition democratic, with employees across the organization able to join in the fun. Not only do customers love it, but so do the front-line staff commenting on workforce-focused sites like Glassdoor and Indeed.

"Merry Christmas to all, and to all a good flight." That was the closing line of the original Christmas-miracle video, which continues to enjoy large viewership four years after being posted. As of the time of this writing, views on YouTube exceed 47 million, leading *Forbes* to comment that the firm has enjoyed "the kind of branding that normally only Santa can deliver."[24]

Closing Thoughts

Throughout the rest of this book, I'll show other examples of how purpose (or lack thereof) affects companies on social media. We'll see how not just customers but employees, former employees, government regulators, citizen watchdogs, and others are controlling the conversation in the way that was formerly controlled by television-advertising buys.

The above examples were no doubt as extremely different as you can get. I provide them as memorable case studies to show four key takeaways:

- The companies that do best in this environment will be the ones who realize that while they can't control the conversation, they can have a significant influence on the raw materials of which it's made.
- The speed of response today is enough to give you whiplash (later in the book, I write in more depth about Pepsi's Kendall Jenner advertisement).
- Purpose is very much tied to the company culture you've committed to building—not the one that's expressed in words on a PowerPoint slide but instead the one expressed by the attitudes and actions of the company's leaders.
- A commitment to purpose will help you to attract and retain people like those from WestJet, who are willing to go the extra mile to thrill your customers.

And that last point might be the perfect way to transition to showing the ways that purpose can help you and your company win the war for talent.

4

Winning the War for Talent

To make the case that purpose can be a strong recruiting tool, I sometimes ask people to imagine a hypothetical job interview. The interviewee is a twenty-eight-year-old woman who is highly motivated and is looking for her next challenge. Sarah is second-generation Indian-American and graduated with highest honors from a prestigious liberal-arts college. She worked for a year at an AIDS hospice in Uganda, got her master of information infrastructure degree from MIT, and then spent four years at Uber building and optimizing its traffic-prediction systems. During that time, she was promoted twice, and by the end she was running a team of fifteen engineers. Intrigued by this candidate? So are hundreds of other firms.

The interviewer charged with closing the deal is our old friend, Professor Milton Friedman. Let's listen in.

FRIEDMAN: Sarah, welcome. Your background and CV are quite impressive. I'd like to start by asking why you want to come work here.

SARAH: Well, sir, with all due respect, I'm not yet certain that I do. The company's financials are impressive, as is the salary offer, and the free daily dog walking is a thoughtful perk little Bowser would love! But there is one thing I've not yet figured out. In your view, what's the social mission here?

FRIEDMAN: Social mission?

SARAH: Yeah—you know, what's the broader purpose of the company?

FRIEDMAN: To return the maximum possible amount of capital to our shareholders.

SARAH: OK, let me try again. Do you see the company having a social obligation to the world?

FRIEDMAN: Young lady, there is one and only one social responsibility of business—to use its resources to engage in activities designed to increase its profits.

So, do you think Professor Friedman closed the deal and landed the prized recruit?

My imaginary interview scenario is admittedly cheeky and perhaps a bit exaggerated, but what the heck, writing a book is a lonely business, and a writer's got to have some fun. Friedman, of course, lived in a different era—one that he helped to create. It was a time when people simply felt lucky to have jobs and moved through their professional lives with the goal of earning a consistent paycheck—not that I blame them. For many, the formative experiences of their lives may have been the Depression, World War II, or the stagflation years of the 1970s, and they therefore placed a premium on predictability and stability. Depending on the age of readers, that might describe parents or grandparents—they'd be a "Ford man" or an "IBM-er" from the day they finished high school or college until that farewell dinner when they collected their gold watch as the sole thank-you for four decades of service.

How quickly things change. Not only are people now much more willing to take risks and switch jobs, but at the same time, the employment market has radically evolved and is so bifurcated that it's like a tale of two cities:

- There are not enough jobs for the mass number of unskilled or less-skilled workers. And unfortunately, every single day, automation and technology will only exacerbate that situation.
- But the opposite is true for the most talented, skilled, and well-educated members of the workforce. Today's most highly sought-after knowledge workers are spoiled for choice. Companies are fighting a perpetual war for talent as they go after the best software coders, the most tenacious salespeople, the most prolific writers, and those who understand rapidly emerging areas of business, ranging from social media to gene sequencing to search-engine optimization.

As a result, many companies trip over themselves to offer higher pay, more equity, and pricey perks, like those famous free meals at Google. But many are overlooking one of the best and newest recruitment tools: purpose.

Will Work for Purpose

"What do I want to do with my life? What am I passionate about? What will my life stand for?" Can you imagine a twenty-eight-year-old working on an assembly line or in a coal mine in Industrial Revolution–era Britain debating the cosmic significance of his life?

Morley Winograd and Michael Hais, coauthors of *Millennial Makeover*, argue that "People born between 1982 and 2000 are the most civic-minded [generation] since the 1930s and 1940s. Other generations were reared to be more individualistic. This civic generation has a willingness to put aside some of their own personal advancement to improve society."

As I researched this book, it wasn't just executives and recruiters regaling me with stories about the challenges they faced in trying to win the war for talent. I also heard stories from parents whose children had recently finished university or graduate school and were sizing up their career options. Perhaps due to pride in their offspring, they'd share how their son or daughter had built the quest for purpose into their screening criteria and the top of their list of questions for every interview. One of my favorites was that of Matt Dee.

Matt was one of those young people thousands of firms want to hire. He was a student of the world, having been raised by American expat parents in Hong Kong and Singapore. He volunteered for numerous causes (including the Room to Read Club at the Singapore American School), had climbed Denali (the highest peak in North America), and had a passion from a young age for computers. He followed that to Carnegie Mellon, where he majored in computer science, with a minor in robotics—with a 3.97 GPA, by the way! He did internships at Square, Palantir, and Dropbox. I asked him about his senior thesis, and he told me he had devised a "Wiki-graph" project: "I designed a system to parse *Wikipedia* and store article relationships in a custom format. It was capable of finding the shortest path between articles in under a second."

Insert image of author scratching his head, smiling, and offering a very lame response of "Wow...cool!"

By the spring of Matt's senior year, firms were lining up to recruit him, and he was juggling dozens of interview opportunities. When the CEO of Stripe calls you personally, you know you're a hot ticket. Was purpose, I asked, something that he included in his due diligence?

> Yes. It was a question I tried to ask at every interview, especially for companies where it is nonobvious what good they provide. I really wanted to work somewhere where people were motivated by what was going on. So, one of my big concerns was not only if the company seemed to have a good goal, but also if the interviewers could articulate it (if not, then maybe it was more of a recruiting pitch, with no internal buy-in?). As interview season wore on, I used this as a filter as I decided which companies to visit for an on-site interview. Due to lack of purpose, for example, I turned down Snapchat after a phone screen.

There's your headline, I thought. Young man turns down opportunity to escape Pittsburgh, in winter, for a free visit to the beaches of Santa Monica and a job opportunity with the hottest pre-IPO company in tech! All due to lack of purpose. Wow...young people sure have changed since the days of my misspent youth! But this is not unusual—one Cone Communications study found that 82 percent of young millennials consider companies' commitments to social causes when deciding which jobs to take.

As he interviewed, the offers rolled in. Two months prior to graduation, he had received offers from big technology firms (including Dropbox, Facebook, Google, Microsoft), start-ups (Affirm, Oscar, Stripe), and a New York–based high-frequency trading firm.

As he began to narrow it down, purpose continued to play a role. He was quite candid that purpose was not the only factor. Matt said:

> I eliminated companies that could not tell me in advance which projects I'd be working on and companies that did not seem like they were poised for significant growth. But as the list got narrower, purpose became a very important screening tool.
>
> I can confidently say that the decision to rule out the high-frequency trading was a purpose question. They paid a lot, had smart people, and I would have learned a ton. But no one could articulate how their

company helped people, or how they had a positive effect on the world. 'Increasing liquidity in the markets' wasn't very convincing," he said with a laugh.

"I would say that Oscar and Stripe were the two companies with the most obvious purpose, so maybe it's not a coincidence that they were my final two. Stripe's CEO tried to sell me based on the purpose angle—helping people from underbanked countries run successful businesses. And then there was Oscar, which I thought had really awesome goals.

Unlike Matt, I had not heard of Oscar, so as we talked, I scrambled to do some quick online research. Oscar, I learned, was a start-up dedicated to fixing the woeful inadequacies of the health-care industry. "Health care is broken," their home page declared. "We're on a mission to fix it. Health-care costs in the US are the highest in the world. But we're not healthier because of it."

Matt was attracted to its goal of creating "a new kind of healthcare company"—one that would put the consumer at the center of everything they did. "It's no secret that dealing with health insurance and health care in the US sucks. People are charged the wrong amounts, you get confusing bills, verbose and confusing explanations of benefits that are hard to read, and it takes a *long* time from seeing a doctor to actually knowing how much you have to pay."

One innovation he loved was the speed, quality, and convenience of response. Let's say, for example, that your child's cough sounds terrible or your knee is in pain or you've just dropped a scalding hot pot of coffee on your foot. Or something more routine—your spouse just reminded you it's been two years since your last physical. Where to begin?

How about this? Open an app. Request an online video chat with a doctor or "health concierge" and then go back to what you were doing. But not for long, because as an Oscar member you've been guaranteed a ten-minute response time. For that burned foot, you're referred to a nearby urgent-care clinic. For the daughter with a cough, a prescription for antibiotics and a strong cough medicine. Or that physical—it's now booked for tomorrow and added to your calendar, and you'll soon receive a text message suggesting some good questions to ask the doctor.

How much did this service just cost you? How about zero? Oscar was the first company to offer free and nearly instantaneous online consultations. And how is this possible? Well, the answer to that question ties into why Matt Dee now works for the company.

The health-care industry, he explained, is overloaded with inefficient systems and processes, all being run on ancient technology. His first job, he said, was replacing a slow and error-prone claims-processing system that was (inside-geek-humor alert) text based and (wait for it...) had been written in COBOL. The inefficiencies of these Stone Age systems resulted in higher costs, which were passed on to consumers.

Better systems, Matt explained, would also lead to better information flow to the consumer. Before you visit your primary-care doctor for your physical or go to the urgent-care clinic for that burned foot, the company would send you a clear summary of the expected cost, how much would be picked up by insurance, and your expected out-of-pocket costs.

Matt could have been helping more teenagers to share more disappearing videos more quickly, but instead, he was part of one of the hottest innovators in health benefits. He was proud that the cost savings driven by the technology he was working on had led to innovations like free medical teleconferencing. "And now," he enthusiastically told me, "many bigger insurers are following us on this. Some competition can go a long way."

The Unlikely Billionaires

One of my favorite stories of a company using purpose to win the war for talent is an Australian software company you've likely never heard of. But given their rate of growth, you likely soon will!

Scott Farquhar and Mike Cannon-Brookes never expected to be taking a company public. In fact, the only thing they considered to be less probable would be becoming billionaires by the age of thirty-five.

And yet on December 1, 2015, they both stood onstage a bit awestruck as they rang the opening bell on the NASDAQ stock exchange. The company they founded after graduating from the University of New South Wales and thwacking $10,000 of debt onto their credit cards—Atlassian—was taken public by the blue-chip investment banks Goldman Sachs and Morgan Stanley.

You might not have heard of Atlassian, as they don't make consumer-facing products like Facebook or Snapchat. Atlassian is a collaboration-software company that helps teams organize, discuss, and complete shared work. More than ninety thousand organizations—including big names like Citigroup, eBay, Coca-Cola, Visa, Procter & Gamble, BMW, and even NASA—use Atlassian's project tracking, collaboration, communication, and development products to work smarter and deliver quality results on time. At a time when, to quote Marc Andreessen, software would "eat the world," the teams at Atlassian are providing some of the best tools in the business to those who wrote and tested that code.

Their customers love the company, and so do their employees. Atlassian continually makes lists of the best places to work—often landing in the top ten. And it turns out that when you ask Scott and Mike the secret to their success, the response will be, "Mate, it's not a secret at all. We've always been very open that we want to be a company that not only produces great products but also makes the world a better place. And we use that, in a big way, as we try to recruit the best and the brightest."

The Starter License: The Little Engine That Could

I first met Mike and Scott and the company's vice president of marketing, Daniel Freeman, at Room to Read's annual Sydney Wine Gala. At the risk of stereotyping, there are few things most Australians like more than relaxing and tossing back a few drinks with their mates. Our 2011 event was the best yet—a full house, the author Bryce Courtney (*The Power of One*) on stage endorsing our work, and a very generous and raucous crowd. It was the first time we had ever raised $1 million in a night in Sydney, and the crowd stayed late to celebrate.

I dropped Daniel, Mike, and Scott an email the next day to thank them for being part of the evening's success. They responded immediately, telling me that they'd had a great time, and they asked if they could get on the phone to pitch an idea.

The three work so well together that they can finish one other's sentences. On our call, they copresented a bold idea:

> We want to offer trial versions of some of our products for potential customers to download online. We think that once they try them, they'll be impressed and then hopefully buy other products from us. It's typical in the software industry to offer free trials. But we think the word *free* can be interpreted as 'not valued.' So instead of free, we are thinking of offering a download of five products, for which we'd charge five dollars. But we won't keep the money—we will donate all five dollars to Room to Read. We will even pay the credit-card processing fees ourselves so that you guys get every penny of the money.

I replied with enthusiasm and asked how many downloads they thought they'd hit.

"We're hoping for five thousand, mate."

"That's great news," I replied. "You'd raise enough funding for us to open five new libraries, serving over two thousand children. Five downloads, five dollars, resulting in five new libraries. Has a nice ring to it, yes?"

Little did we know how much we had underestimated the campaign's potential.

The promotion quickly went viral. Just as with WestJet, when people see companies doing great things, they're often excited and motivated to share that with their networks. Hyperconnected geeks around the world were posting the campaign everywhere from Reddit to Twitter to Facebook. The leaders called their team together to ask, "Should we end the promotion here, now that we've hit the goal?" Their team responded, "Why stop a good thing that's continuing to ramp up and that's helping kids?" Scott pointed out that more new customers would mean more support calls, increasing the burden on teams that were already working extreme hours. The team vowed to work harder. Democracy carried the day, and the promotion continued.

On my next trip to Sydney, Daniel suggested I address the troops at a town-hall meeting. My reward for showing up: an oversize check—for $1 million! The team went crazy with excitement as it learned exactly how much the campaign had overachieved on its original goal.

All in a Day's Work

It's not unusual for Atlassian employees to see a guy like me dropping by their offices to say thanks. From the beginning, the company made a commitment to develop great software and do great things for the world. It made an early pledge that 1 percent of its profits would be given to worthy causes and that 1 percent of its equity would be irrevocably placed in a foundation. Scott joked to me that "1 percent of nothing was nothing back then, so it was relatively easy to do," but today that foundation has almost US$50 million to deploy. Employees are given five days off per year to volunteer their time for good causes, and the company will give their software away to nonprofits (over fifty-four thousand licenses donated to date).

The cofounders were always committed to using the power of business to do good things for the world, but one day they decided that it should be democratized throughout the company. Scott told me, "From day one, Mike and I knew we wanted to have an impact on the world beyond the software we were building. In the early days, it was Mike and I giving to causes that meant something to us, to causes that were close to our hearts. But then we realized, as Atlassian grew, it was bigger than just us. We wanted to create an environment where everyone could give back to causes they believed in too."

The company's core values have evolved to reflect these beliefs. Their first value—and the one that's most famous—is both direct and simple: "Open company. *No bullshit.*" Employees are encouraged to "be the change you seek" and to have "the courage and resourcefulness to spark change." Ego and self-promotion are discouraged, with teamwork being a core value. The "Company Values" page of the Atlassian website states, "We spend a huge amount of our time at work. So, the more that time doesn't feel like 'work,' the better."

Daniel, Mike, and Scott often shared with me that while they enjoyed doing good for their community and the wider world, they had seen massive and not entirely expected business benefits from the firm's larger sense of purpose.

Great Code Doesn't Write Itself

Scott explained to me over a harborside sushi dinner how purpose has proven to be a big competitive advantage for Atlassian.

We face several challenges in recruiting. We're not a household name. We're recruiting not only in Sydney but also in other cities where we've opened offices like Amsterdam, Austin, and San Francisco. We're not very well known in those places, but we're growing like mad and trying to recruit the best engineers and other tech professionals. After all, great code does not write itself. We're competing against the likes of Google, Facebook, Twitter, LinkedIn, Expedia, Uber, and dozens of others, and we need a way to differentiate ourselves.

We've managed to recruit some of the best people in the business. I personally talk to every single new hire, and I ask them, 'Why did you decide to come work for us?' And I'll tell you, the number one answer—and number two is not even close—is that they liked that our company has a strong sense of purpose. Most of our new hires tell me that they know that by building this company, we're doing great things for the world through our charity partners.

Scott's belief is echoed by the executive responsible for the hiring surge. One HR executive described the company's focus on values as critical to recruiting the best people and opined, "I think in some ways that does give us an unfair advantage—we have done such a good job of weaving our values to the business model itself that we keep it front and center in everything we do."[25]

Robert Allen, the company's global head of talent acquisition, shared with me his belief that "many companies talk about the values as being important, but I can truly say that we are held accountable to them day in, day out. For me personally, they are a great North Star in the recruiting of the next chapter of talent for Atlassian."

Mike and Scott have encouraged the team to have values and purpose permeate every part of the business. "We want people to know, even during the interview process, that this is not a company that treats doing social good as a department or something we do on an annual 'day of service.' No way, mate. Here at Atlassian, it's not one day—it's every day, and it comes straight from the top, and it's something we ask every employee to think about every day and co-own with us."

Here's What a Highly Motivated Team Looks Like

Atlassian, which employs more than two thousand people in twelve cities, has twice been voted the best place to work in Australia—the only company to have enjoyed back-to-back wins. They've also earned a top-ten spot on *Fortune*'s global list of the "Ten Best Workplaces in Tech." Scott views purpose as being a key reason for that success. He told me in one of our many conversations, "We have this engaged workforce who come to work every day and feel like they're giving back in everything they do."

As the company continues to grow, Mike and Scott shared that their biggest goal for the company was to keep its values and the culture strong. "If we have a group of people who want to come to work every day—that's what makes us win."

Those employees also stick around. Attrition rates at Atlassian are well below the average for the software field, with one HR executive saying they are "half of what I have experienced in my career" prior to being at Atlassian.[26]

As I'll posit throughout this book, the benefits of purpose are often not limited to just one part of the business. I could have used Atlassian as an example in the customer chapter, as many now-loyal customers began with the Starter License being their first experience with Atlassian's software. And once they've joined the family, they've then bought significant numbers of additional applications. Mike was hesitant to reveal the exact figure for competitive reasons but told me that it was "in the tens of millions." In the software business, when someone pays you for a download of a piece of code over the Internet, the gross margins are as close to 100 percent as its possible to get. Atlassian also uses purpose not just to recruit employees but to also keep them motivated. Their annual trip to visit Room to Read's work in Cambodia, as an example, is wildly popular and fills up every year within a few days of being announced.

Meanwhile, on the Fund-Raising Front

The Atlassian Starter License campaign was a huge success. Atlassian has provided over $6 million in funding for Room to Read and now contributes $1 million per year. The company has become one of Room to Read's single largest sources of funding and the largest investor in our work in Cambodia. Every year twenty employees who are highly engaged with the Atlassian Foundation receive the ultimate perk: a four-day trip to Cambodia to meet the children, families, and communities whose lives they're impacting. Over 250,000 students in this formerly war-ravaged country have access to our programs—all because three guys at a very young start-up decided to launch a purpose-driven innovation and to not view purpose as being an enemy of profit.

The Zero-Emissions Pitch

I see purpose popping up more often as a recruiting tool, especially with companies trying to recruit millennials. The courier service Postmates, which promises "On demand, 7/24, the best of your city," is reengineering business deliveries. Around the world, the way we move things from point A to point B is undergoing radical change. Whether it's those moving people (Uber, Lyft, bike-share programs), physical goods (Amazon, TaskRabbit, UPS, FedEx), or your next meal (Blue Apron, UberEats, Deliveroo, Foodpanda), the race is on to acquire customers and to gain early market share.

Critical to that mission is to have enough drivers, especially during periods of surging demand. Postmates, as one example, was on a huge recruiting push as it rapidly expanded to over two hundred American cities, in places as small as Belle Meade, Tennessee, and Bethany, Oklahoma. And they incorporated purpose into their pitch. The online advertisement that had impressed me carried the headline "Ride a Postmates Zero-Emissions Scooter," just above a very modern-looking and aerodynamic two-wheeler. The advert went on to encourage the potential applicant to "promote sustainability" in his or her career decisions.

MBAs Join the Migration

This migration is not just happening with entry-level courier drivers but even among MBAs—a cohort that in the past has been ridiculed as being avaricious and focused on nothing more than feathering its own nest. But according to Net Impact, a coalition of social-impact clubs with a presence on over one hundred campuses, and its 2014 Business as *Un*usual study, 83 percent of MBAs say they want to have a job that seeks to make a difference in the world either socially or environmentally.

As an example, Louis Dorval is a Canadian who received his MBA at Oxford (with a scholarship from the Skoll Foundation) and now lives in Massachusetts. He took a break from Viamo, his mobile-phone communication and survey platform (a "tech start-up slash social enterprise") to tell me, "I went to business school to understand how to create business models around the positive impact I wanted to have in Africa. I chose a program specialized in social entrepreneurship because growing organizations with a double bottom line have unique challenges and because I wanted to grow my relationship network in this field."

The growth of for-good versus for-profit projects like the one Dorval was working on comes at a moment of shifting priorities in business education. An increasing number of MBA students are sidestepping the traditional post–business school career path in favor of professional trajectories that give back.

A 2015 study by Bain & Company of some fifteen hundred MBA students and graduates found that the clear majority intend to prioritize "impact" over prestige and financial gains in their careers.

"The millennials, whether they articulate it or not, want to be part of something larger than themselves," said Shlomo "Solly" Angel, a professor at NYU's Marron Institute of Urban Planning. "And we [as schools] are not just about creating the next generation of profit-maximizing business leaders."[27]

But it's not just the underthirties who hear the siren call of purpose.

"My Wife Is Going to Kill Me"

Scott Ullem did not want to fly out to Orange County, California, for the interview. But the headhunter kept pushing him, asking him, "Why can't you just jump on the plane and go check it out?" *It* was a new job opportunity. The CFO position at Edwards Lifesciences, she told him, was the perfect fit.

Scott, forty-six at the time, had already had two distinct phases of his career: banking at Goldman Sachs and Merrill Lynch, followed by the CFO position at Bemis, one of the world's largest manufacturers of extruded plastic products. He was not looking for any opportunity that involved moving down the street, let alone halfway across the country. Just five years earlier, he and his wife, Beth, had moved themselves and their three children from Chicago to Neenah, Wisconsin. Their youngest, a son with heart issues, had made the rough transition to a whole new medical team. Mac's older siblings, John and Caroline, had made their own transitions to a new school. Everything was as stable in the family's life as it had been in a long time. As Scott hung up the phone, he thought, We need another family move like we need a hole in the head.

And yet he was intrigued by the opportunity. Edwards Lifesciences was searching for their next CFO. The company is the leading maker of heart valves in the world, which was outside Scott's comfort zone. This could be a very interesting switch. But what the hell did he know about medical technology?

Against his better judgment, he agreed to fly out to talk about the opportunity, assuring his wife that there was no way in the world it would work out anyway—only to end up in an interview that changed his life.

Meet the Team Who Saved Your Life

In Scott's words:

"So, I'm walking across this beautiful campus, basking in sunshine and eighty-degree temperatures. A nice contrast to the near-perpetual ice I left behind in northern Wisconsin.

"My final interview was with the guy who would be my boss if I joined: the CEO. Mike [Mussallem] had been in the role for fourteen years. One thing that intrigued me was the fact that over three hundred thousand times a year, the company was helping to prolong or even save the life of a person who might otherwise have died. I visualized all those spouses, all those children and grandchildren, who would get to enjoy many more years with their loved one.

"I also learned that Edwards had a large and diverse workforce because the precision required to guarantee both fit and duration for the valve is such that it cannot be done by machine. Only human hands—ideally small and delicate ones—can do the trick. Many of those workers were first- or second-generation immigrants—mostly women—from countries like the Philippines and Indonesia.

"Mike and I talked a lot about business matters, the usual stuff that a potential CFO would talk to a CEO about. And near the end of our allotted time, I asked him, 'For you, what's the best part of working here?'

"'That's easy,' Mike replied. 'Let me tell you about the days when a patient and their family arrive on campus. Those are the best days we have, when we see how our hard work pays off. Oftentimes, they bring their spouse; sometimes they bring a collection of kids and even grandkids. Imagine an elderly patient walking in the front door and saying, "Good morning. I have one of your devices in here [gestures toward his heart]. I am wondering if I can meet the people who sewed my valve."

"'The receptionist offers a warm welcome and a friendly smile, then leaps immediately into action—the company has had this happen enough times that there is a standard procedure she can rely on. Behind the scenes, there has been work to identify the team who worked on the patient's valve, utilizing a unique serial number that identifies not only the materials used in the valve but also the individual employees who utilized a microscope, specialized needle, and medical-grade thread to hand-sew thousands of stitches to assemble each valve. They have received the call that all employees who work in this role eagerly await in their careers at Edwards: a patient has come to visit. They want to meet their "makers."

"'Ten minutes later, a group walks into the waiting room to greet the patient and his family as the receptionist tells them, "These are the people who hand-sewed your valve."

"'Next thing you know, they're hugging,' Mike recalls. 'The former patient, the Edwards employees, his wife. They're crying. There are photographs, more hugs, hand holding, and the sharing of personal stories. Often it's more than just the three—a lot of valve-disease survivors bring their children and grandchildren with them. They make it a family pilgrimage. Nothing is more incredible—to have a patient put their arm around you, put your hand on their heart, and say, "I'm here because of you"…that stays with you for a lifetime.'

Scott asked Mike how often this happened. "Several times a month. I see them all the time. After the reunion, our team often gives them a tour of the facilities, and sometimes they'll stop by my office."

Scott stops. The pause is quite long. It seems obvious to me that he's told this story many dozens of times but that each time is like the first time, and it will never get old.

"And so there I am, holding back tears as I hear this story. Mike has tears in his eyes, and so do I, and all I was thinking was, OK, I'm in. I need to come work here.

"And let me tell you, I'm over a year into working in this environment. The move was not easy, but it's done, and now my life is completely different. Every conversation our team has is about what's best for our patients. The most meaningful statistics I look at as the CFO are not about cash flow, but about the quality and reliability of our devices.

"I can tell you one thing about the entire future of my career: when it comes to having purpose as part of each and every day on the job, *there's no going back!*"

Bringing Your Whole Self to Work

The smartest and most agile companies are hearing these preferences loud and clear and building purpose into their recruiting strategies and pitches.

A great example is Salesforce. Since its founding in 1999, the company has grown so quickly that it's basically never stopped recruiting. They're competing for the best and the brightest in the white-hot Bay Area market. So how have they recruited over twenty thousand employees? I knew some of their first recruits, and they always cited the firm's commitment to the one-one-one model, under which a written pledge was made that 1 percent of the firm's equity, annual profits, and employee hours would be dedicated to working toward improving the state of the world. And it turns out that purpose plays an outsize role in their recruiting strategy.

Suzanne DiBianca is the firm's chief philanthropy officer. In a talk at the annual convening of the World Economic Forum in Davos, she enlightened the audience with the company's approach: "What we notice about the attraction of talent is, particularly with the next generation, there is a very blurred line between work and life—they really just want to bring their whole selves to work. And so they expect from their company that they are going to be good corporate citizens and do good in the world, as well as conducting their business."

I take everything Salesforce says about recruiting seriously. After all, despite being in a white-hot and highly competitive recruiting market, they've become the largest private employer in San Francisco. The soon-to-be-completed Salesforce Tower will be the city's tallest building. All those floors require a lot of talented people. When I asked Suzanne over dinner how they've been so successful when competing against everyone from Facebook to Google to Uber, she immediately emphasized that they make sure each interviewee knows about the one-one-one commitment.

We tell them this means they can actually enjoy paid days off for volunteering for causes they love. They can nominate those organizations to get access to free or discounted software and storage in the cloud. We even help to make the sector more efficient by having our employees help to optimize and troubleshoot their IT and donor-management systems. It's a very powerful combination when we tell them they don't have to think of it as a trade-off, that they can work for us while also spending time with causes they believe in. We don't just tolerate it—we actively encourage it and even track it.

Founder Marc Benioff provides further confirmation of the model. He told *Fast Company* that "Salesforce gives guidance to our employees to get out there and volunteer, and I think that's why we have high levels of satisfaction in our employees and why we can attract people. We are creating an environment that gives them satisfaction in their work, not just financial gains."[28]

These promises are worth contemplating for a moment. To combine profits with passion and purpose. To be not just allowed but encouraged to bring your whole selves to work. Appealing? It must be to a lot of people, as the company has grown to twenty-six thousand employees and will add over five thousand more in the next three years—and all this in the ultracompetitive San Francisco technology sector.

Without Fear or Favor

Eager to learn whether other companies were seeing similar conditions in the current recruiting environment, I had drinks with *Financial Times* CEO John Ridding. Ridding started as a reporter at the *Financial Times*, was later publisher for the Asian region, and became global CEO in 2007:

> The types of people you want to win over have an increasingly different approach to choosing the organizations they want to be part of. It all ties to vision, mission, values, and purpose. You can look back at what it was

like for our fathers and how quickly that's changed. Our parents' generation wanted a regular and predictable salary. Now the game has changed. For me as a CEO, I must get involved personally, and it's all about, how do we persuade you to come work for us?

As we talked over dinner, I reminded John of a recent meeting I'd had with some of the top leaders at Egon Zehnder, a firm whose one-thousand-plus recruiters spend a lot of time thinking about these issues. A report they'd given me as required reading had echoed Ridding: "We have learned that the war for talent is real. And businesses that can show a higher sense of purpose have a much better chance of winning this war."

And how does Ridding do that? Partly by reminding recruits that one of the most effective ways to pressure the business community, financial firms, and governments to act in an ethical manner is a strong, independent, and fearless press: "The eternal purpose of the *FT*, through the years and across all formats (print, digital, etc.) is to deliver high-quality independent journalism, globally, without fear or favor. And I'd reckon that everyone at the *FT* knows that. It's a unifying force. 'Without Fear or Favour' is written on our masthead."

Ridding also cites the *Financial Times*' annual seasonal appeal as an effective method of appealing to recruits. Given the financial demographic of their readership (spoiler alert: really rich!), each year the company's employees perform due diligence on well-run charities and, through a staff vote, select one to be the recipient of reader contributions through a month-long seasonal appeal. Journalists venture into the field to witness the work being done by groups like Doctors without Borders, SightSavers, and the International Rescue Committee and share the inspiring stories of change with *Financial Times* readers. Staff also host fund-raising events and share the appeal on social media.

Ridding told me, "It's such a powerful story to share with recruits—that every December they'll be helping to fund a great cause, and they're not doing it through pocket change or bake sales but rather by leveraging our readership to raise literally millions of dollars that will be used to help refugees, to build schools, or to prevent blindness."

When Purpose Snowballs

Ridding's approach illustrates what happens when executives listen to market feedback. Deloitte's survey of the most-connected millennials found that 78 percent value working for an employer that is socially and/or environmentally responsible. Since they're the most connected generation in human history, their views on their employers spread quickly. Friends on social media will quickly know whether working for Company X is inspiring or an "energy suck" to be avoided at all costs. In the same way they review a restaurant on Yelp or a hotel on Trip Advisor, they'll anonymously report to the wider world on their experience as an employee on sites like Glassdoor.

This can be a double-edged sword, so the challenge for every leader is to make sure employees are inspired enough to "recruit, not repel" potential employees. John Ridding told me, "When we hire a good person, we know that if they have a positive initial experience, then they will attract other good people. So, this whole area of mission and purpose—I don't consider it to be soft stuff—I think it's a big deal."

The quest to find meaning in work is not limited to only one age. As millions of seasoned businesspeople like Scott Ullem pursue purpose-driven careers, they'll be able to recruit from their networks. Talent attracts talent, and when your employee is doing the job of a recruitment agency but at zero cost, that's a huge benefit to both the top line and the bottom.

Kristin Richmond and Kirsten Tobey have had to recruit quickly to keep up with their annual revenue growth of 30 percent. Starting with just six employees in Oakland in 2006, they've grown the company to over seventeen hundred employees. They cite one simple strategy to recruit top-notch talent: "Creating and maintaining a clear vision for the company."[29]

A Two-Way Street

Vicky Tsai can attest to this: "Purpose comes up a lot in interviews. There are lots of different start-ups here in San Francisco and Silicon Valley. Sometimes people will choose a start-up because they think they're going on a big money run. Others will choose a certain company because they want to associate with that value system. When we recruit we're looking for people who share our value system. They can be any shape, size, color, or skill set if the values are in sync. So, when they mention it in an interview, which they usually do these days, it's an indicator to us that we're talking to someone who cares about the same things that we do."

NiQ Lai expressed similar beliefs: "At HKBN, we look at a corporate version of Maslow's pyramid, with money being at the bottom, and purpose being at the top. Once a company has established itself beyond the basic survival level—i.e., with enough money to feed itself—we can then choose to compete at the bottom or the top of the pyramid. If we want the absolute best people, people with passion in addition to ability, then we must appeal to their higher Maslow need for purpose.

> In business, they say that if you pay peanuts, you will get monkeys. If you pay with just more peanuts—i.e., just more money—you will simply get bigger monkeys. To attract absolutely the best talents—we refer to employees as "talents"—we must appeal to a common purpose. This is what we try to do with our core purpose of 'Make our Hong Kong a better place to live.' If you love this core purpose, come join us. But if the purpose is meaningless to you, please join our competitors.

Elon Musk: Winning the War for Talent on Three Fronts

If recruiting the most talented people in the world to join your firm were an Olympic sport, it's likely that Elon Musk would be wearing multiple gold medals. Musk is best known as the founder of Tesla, but—never one to rest—he has also played key roles in founding and running two other cutting-edge companies: SpaceX and Solar City. One of the most famous entrepreneurs in the world, Musk was little known before 2012. He was one of six PayPal cofounders, but it was only when his next big bets began to prosper that the world took notice. As described in his biography by author Ashlee Vance:

> [By then his] companies were succeeding at unprecedented things. SpaceX flew a supply capsule to the International Space Station and brought it safely back to Earth. Tesla Motors delivered the Model S, a beautiful, all-electric sedan that took the automotive industry's breath away and slapped Detroit sober. These two feats elevated Musk to the rarest heights among business titans. Only Steve Jobs could claim similar achievements in two such different industries, sometimes putting out a new Apple product and a blockbuster Pixar movie in the same year. And yet, Musk was not done. He was also the chairman and largest shareholder of SolarCity, a booming solar energy company poised to file for an initial public offering. Musk had somehow delivered the biggest advances the space, automotive, and energy industries had seen in decades in what felt like one fell swoop.[30]

Musk was driven to focus his next initiatives on something bigger than padding his own nest. In a 2012 Caltech commencement address, he told students that after leaving PayPal he asked himself the question, "What are some of the other problems that are likely to most affect the future of humanity? Not from the perspective, 'What's the best way to make money?' which is OK, but it was really, 'What do I think is going to most affect the future of humanity?'" He was eager to apply innovation to the areas "that will most affect our future" and eventually embraced not just one challenge but three: "I am committed to finding renewable energy solutions, accelerating the adoption of sustainable transportation, and revolutionizing space travel."[31]

Mission as a Magnet

I wrote earlier about how the current hiring market is insanely competitive at the top end of the market for those with the most skills and experience. Musk is, of course, trying to land the top tier of the top 1 percent. After all, you can't move human beings safely to the planet Mars or design an all-electric vehicle capable of going from zero to sixty in four seconds without the most talented designers, coders, engineers, and testers on the planet. To win the war for talent at one cutting-edge company would be a real coup. To do it at three simultaneously would be completely unprecedented.

And yet Musk is doing exactly that. How? It turns out that having a world-changing purpose as part of the company's raison d'être plays a very big role. Let's look briefly at how each of these three companies frames its mission on its website:

- **Tesla:** "Tesla was founded...by a group of engineers...who wanted to prove that electric cars could be better than gasoline-powered cars. With instant torque, incredible power, and zero emissions, Tesla's products would be cars without compromise. Each new generation would be increasingly affordable, helping the company work toward its mission: to accelerate the world's transition to sustainable energy."
- **SpaceX:** "SpaceX designs, manufactures, and launches advanced rockets and spacecraft. The company was founded in 2002 to revolutionize space technology, with the goal of enabling people to live on other planets."
- **SolarCity:** "SolarCity is America's top full-service solar provider. We make clean energy available to [customers] at a lower cost than they pay for energy generated by burning fossil fuels like coal, oil, and natural gas...We've revolutionized the way energy

is delivered by giving customers a cleaner, more affordable alternative to their monthly utility bill."

There's nothing in here about market share, EPS, or maximizing cash returns to shareholders. The company's missions are audacious and—if successful—world changing. And it turns out that that can attract a lot of talent.

Building the A-Team at Tesla

When Musk set out to disrupt the old guard, he framed the company's mission as a revolutionary quest that would change the world. He saw the car's potential to transform the perception of electric cars from something ugly and slow and boring to sexy and aspirational. He preached the benefits of solar, selling the vision of replacing every belching gas guzzler with a zero-emissions vehicle. For the consumer, every solar fill-up would be free. For the benefit of the world, tens of billions of dollars would no longer end up in the hands of petro-dictator states like Iran, Saudi Arabia, and Venezuela.

He also appealed to the rational engineers' mind-set. So much solar energy hits the surface of the Earth every hour that it's equal to a year's worth of worldwide energy consumption from all sources put together. So why not make the switch from coal, nuclear, and petroleum? *Solar energy is there for the taking, so let's design a smart system to take it!*

The pitch worked! As one example of the talent that flocked to Musk's companies, I present Gene Berdichevsky. He was a valued team member at Stanford's solar-powered-car team but quickly became a flight risk once he heard of Tesla's plans. He volunteered to quit school, work for free, and sweep the floors at Tesla if that's what it took to get a job there. He became employee number seven (spoiler alert: he's not currently carrying a broom, and he's being well compensated).

Taking Aim at "Success without Significance"

As Musk recruited for all three companies, he took direct aim at the Silicon Valley firms with whom he was competing for talent, pointing out that many of them were more driven by profits than by purpose. Musk bemoaned that throughout the tech industry, once lofty and idealistic ambitions had been dumbed down. "The goals had changed—from taking huge risks to create new industries and grand new ideas to chasing easier money by entertaining consumers and pumping out simple apps and advertisements."[32] "I think there are probably too many smart people pursuing Internet stuff, finance, and law. That is part of the reason why we haven't seen as much innovation.

Or as Jeffrey Hammerbacher, an early Facebook employee, once famously opined, "The best minds of my generation are thinking about how to make people click ads. That sucks."

Praise from Page

When your competitors extol you, you know you must be doing something right. Google cofounder Larry Page is competing for talent on multiple fronts with Musk's companies. While nobody could accuse Google of thinking small—after all, they're pursuing everything from self-driving cars to robots to finding ways to help people live to be 150 (and a healthy 150 at that)—Page praises Musk for the radical and world-changing goals that his companies are built around. He also posits that this is a competitive advantage in hiring the best and the brightest:

If you think about Silicon Valley or corporate leaders in general, they're not usually lacking in money. If you have all this money, which presumably you're going to give away and couldn't even spend it all if you wanted to, why then are you devoting your time to a company that's not really doing anything good? That's why I find Elon to be an inspiring example. He said, "Well, what should I really do in this world? Solve cars, global warming, and make humans multiplanetary." I mean those are compelling goals, and now he has businesses to do that. This becomes a competitive advantage for him, too. Why would you want to work for a defense contractor when you can work for a guy who wants to go to Mars, and he's going to move heaven and earth to make it happen? [He] can frame a problem in a way that's really good for the business.

Are You in It to Win It?

Not every one of us can be Elon Musk—but that's no reason not to internalize the lessons we can learn from him. It's critical to remember that we are all increasingly competing against companies like his when it comes to winning the affections of customers, creating a social-media buzz, winning the war for talent, and keeping our best people highly motivated to minimize flight risk. As an example, GM chair Mary Barra has thirty-three thousand followers on Twitter. Musk has more than four hundred times that number: 13.6 million.

It's not just Musk's companies—it's also hundreds of B Corps and other companies, like Atlassian, Oscar, Edwards Lifesciences, and Salesforce, who have already incorporated and deeply embedded purpose into their business model and culture. With more leaders and more organizations using purpose to help win the war for talent, we ignore examples like these at our own peril.

Having a strong sense of purpose is no guarantee that you will win the war for talent. You still have to offer a competitive salary and benefits package, prove to the recruit that your company has a compelling customer-value proposition, and treat employees fairly. But lack of purpose is almost certain to increasingly put you further behind the most attractive companies. If you're not able to make a compelling case that the recruit will work in a place imbued with a strong sense of purpose, you'll likely find yourself in that same position our hypothetical Professor Friedman did at the beginning of this chapter. You'll be going back to square one as you hear the words,

"Sorry, but I got a better offer."

Not only do you have to recruit great people, you also, of course, must keep them motivated and retain those who are performing at the highest level. So, we will next look at how purpose is doing exactly that at more and more companies.

5

Motivate Your Employees, and Retain Your Superstars

There's lots of *talk* about keeping employees happy. We read about free lunches, napping pods, and year-end bonuses, but the day-to-day reality is that employee morale is an afterthought at most companies. "Yes, yes, it's important," many managers think to themselves, "and I'll get to it just as soon as we sort out *x, y,* and *z*." It's on the to-do list, for sure, but it's toward the bottom of the second page.

Part of the problem is that companies don't appreciate the importance of employee motivation and retention until it's too late. Losing an employee isn't just a bummer. It's not simply a drain on the human-resources department. There are massive repercussions, and if more managers understood the math more clearly, they wouldn't be so quick to relegate employee satisfaction to that second page.

The other part of the problem is that—even if you were to grasp its importance—you have no clue how to manage the issue. For many, employee motivation and retention are a mystery. You've built a good product, you're paying a good wage, you're pleasant in the hallway. Hell, you even learned to fist-bump to connect with those tattooed millennial employees. And yet so many keep leaving "for greener pastures." What more can you do?

Additionally, unlike with customers, whose enthusiasm can be quantified in terms of sales, repeat business, and market share, it's much harder to measure the happiness level of workers. The result is that managers go fumbling about in the dark, choosing to either bury their heads in the sand or order a beer-pong table from Amazon.

Before we talk about the solution, let's make sure we understand the problem.

Houston, We Have a (Motivation) Problem

Less than one-third of US employees are engaged at work, according to the gold-standard Gallup survey data of the American workforce. Globally, the rate is a staggeringly low 13 percent. Over the past decade, these dismal numbers have barely budged; dissatisfaction and disengagement are not a trend—they're the reality year in and year out.

We're not just talking about staff on the bottom rungs of the ladder. Gallup also surveyed 2.5 million manager-led teams in 195 countries and found that—get ready for this—half of all managers are not engaged, and a further 14 percent are actively disengaged.

Ouch.

Purpose to the Rescue

I spend a lot of time talking to people about their businesses—from unknown start-ups to globe-spanning banks. A constant subject of conversation is how they keep their best people highly motivated. Financial incentives—an increase in salary, an annual performance-based bonus—tend to produce a bit of a "sugar high." Employees are temporarily elated, but after a few weeks, the increased compensation is "the new normal" and all too quickly taken for granted. So many of them have added purpose into the mix—and seen great results in motivation.

Let's now look at how two vastly different organizations are using purpose to motivate their people.

"We Give People a Second Chance to Live Their Whole Lives"

I checked in with Scott Ullem a year after he started at Edwards Lifesciences. "Has it proven to be true, I asked, that the workplace is as motivating as your CEO Mike had told you it would be?" When he responded in the affirmative, I took the opportunity to ask if there was any statistical proof. As Edward Deming once said, "In God we trust. All others bring data."

Scott connected me with Gina Codd, an Edwards vice president of human resources, who very generously shared internal studies on employee motivation.

Gina shared a 2016 Edwards study that asked manufacturing employees to evaluate the importance of various attributes of their jobs. "The thing I found most interesting," she shared, was that "manufacturing employees, who earn hourly wages, rated product quality and patient focus as among the most important attributes of working at Edwards." Indeed, these two factors were chosen nearly 70 percent of the time as being among the five most important attributes to these associates. Gina shared that "it's interesting, when you think of Maslow's hierarchy of needs, that both were chosen in the top five more often than more self-centered attributes including vacation, stability, and work-life balance."

Even among the manufacturing associates who had the lowest engagement scores and were thus the highest "flight risk," the importance of patient focus and product quality still received high scores.

The strong sense of purpose also plays a strong role in keeping the professional-level employees strongly motivated. Another 2016 study asked professional employees if they would stay at Edwards if they were offered a comparable position with similar pay and benefits at another company. Of employees who responded positively for staying, company growth, patient focus, and product quality were selected as the top three reasons.

Gina also shared with me her experiences, which were very similar to what Scott had told me: "One of the most moving experiences is when we bring patients in, and we trace their heart valve back to the actual employees that made it, and they all get to meet. Tears of joy are guaranteed!"

Having now heard about these patient reunions on multiple occasions, I wanted to witness them myself. Sure, it sounded good when the CEO and the vice president of human resources talked about it. But what, I wondered, was it like for those front-line employees?

Thankfully, Edwards was willing to give me that opportunity. Jerry Robinson, a seventy-one-year-old Californian, and his wife, Myrna, had been invited to visit the firm's Singapore plant. During their tour they looked through a window into the "clean room," as word spread across the floor: "That's him! That's Mr. Jerry!" The workers quickly put down their sewing to greet Jerry and Myrna by placing their hands together, making virtual hearts, and raising them to their chests.

That first round of tears was soon replaced by a second, at the in-person reunion. Jerry told the group how abruptly his life had changed. A long-time runner, he had completed every Los Angeles Marathon since its inception—twenty-nine in all. But one day, as he walked to the start line of a five-kilometer race, he had a very serious shortness of breath. It did not go away—soon he was not able to even walk up to their house's single flight of stairs without stopping to catch his breath. The first doctor Jerry consulted told him he'd never run another marathon. He got not just a second opinion but five of them and was soon on the operating table at UCLA Medical Center. The surgery went so well that he was out walking within twenty-four hours of leaving the ICU. Within a month his cardiologist gave approval for Jerry to resume marathon training.

Through teary eyes, Jerry told the Edwards workers gathered with him in Singapore, "Before the procedure, I could not even walk across the street. You have turned my life around." He then shared that they had helped him to defy earlier predictions—just a few months earlier, he had once again completed the Los Angeles Marathon!

The heart-valve team at Edwards was just as excited and even more emotional. I scrambled to write down its thoughts on the reunion.

"I'm so excited. My heart valve that I sewed last year—it's inside him. This touched my heart."

"I feel wonderful. We actually give people a second chance to live their whole life."

"I got the chance to meet my patient, and it made me feel amazing and proud of what we've done. What we do is so important. It's not just work—it's work that saves lives."

"My work is quite tiring, but after meeting Mr. Jerry, I feel like it's worth it."

"Before, I thought my job was just a simple one. But then I met this person, and I think it's so special that I saved his life."

Now I understood why Scott had told me that for him, "There's no going back!"

Sharing the Gold at Goldman

Not all companies have purpose baked into their product offering as clearly as Edwards does. But more and more are finding that there's an incentive to utilize purpose as a way to motivate and retain their best people.

I ran across an interesting innovation in this area through a friend in the Tokyo office of Goldman Sachs. While the firm sometimes gets a bad rap in the global media, it's actually deploying a lot more philanthropic dollars than most people realize (it's historically been very quiet about it). In fact, in 2010 the firm's management committee made a decision to reduce the partner-compensation pool by a certain percentage and donate that amount of money into a new philanthropic fund called Goldman Sachs Gives. From there, the firm's partners have the chance to recommend grants to nonprofit organizations. Considering that bonuses are the vast majority of its annual compensation, this pot of money was bound to be substantial. This mandatory contribution toward a better world would be held in what's called a donor-advised fund, with the partner then deciding which worthy causes to support. This new innovation was not optional but mandatory; it was strongly reinforced by CEO Lloyd Blankfein himself. If you were a partner, you would now be giving away a lot of money every year.

Since the program started, more than a billion dollars has been deployed to over 5,700 organizations! It was always at the discretion of the partner and often his or her spouse. But at a certain point, one executive connected the dots and asked, "Why should we partners have all the fun?" The firm began encouraging its analysts (mostly fresh out of college) to form "pitch teams" that competed for donations to one of their favorite causes. The winners would be chosen by a judging panel of senior executives. At stake: grants of $100,000 for first place and $50,000 and $25,000 for the silver- and bronze-medal winners.

I wanted to learn more about the origins of the new Analyst Impact Fund challenge, so I reached out to the firm's global head of human-capital management, Edith Cooper. How, I asked, was the decision made to involve the analysts in allocating so much charitable capital? Here's her answer:

> As a management committee, we hold ourselves accountable for understanding the environment that our people desire and how we can enhance and promote the culture, which of course expands to our impact on the broader population. At an off-site we talked about the analyst experience and how we really wanted to understand the environment and what people were really looking for in the workplace today. GS Gives is incredibly important to us, and during the conversations, one of our partners put the pieces together and said, "We're hearing from our analysts that they want to make an impact, so let's give them the opportunity to bring forward causes they care about." Great ideas come from collaboration and dialogue, and this is a good example of that.

Edith told me that the idea was immediately embraced and that the conversation shifted very quickly to implementation. The management committee was not the only place it was a popular idea; news of the opportunity spread like wildfire among the analysts. Pitch teams quickly assembled among causes ranging from using data science to solve social issues to using trained rats to remove land mines to girls' education to the refugee crisis. Edith gave me her insider's view of the first round of proposals and pitches:

> It was very exciting. The finalist teams presented to the partnership committee, some members of the management committee, and even Lloyd was there. It was so impressive—seeing the presentation skills, the selling skills, and advocacy that was required to get buy-in. The excitement in the room was just incredible.

I asked Edith about some of those elements. For example, does it help to get a young employee to put down the pitch books and the spreadsheets and to instead work on presentation skills that might later be useful in future roles with the firm? She agreed and shared some of the other benefits she saw: "It was extraordinary for community building. That was one other really great thing about it— when you looked at the teams, they were often geographically dispersed. It was amazing to see an analyst in Mexico City working with another in Frankfurt, and we had others in New York, Bengaluru, and London, just to name a few of the offices."

Goldman Sachs also found, just as we saw in the last chapter, that initiatives like these were also helpful to the recruiting process. We talked by phone as she was en route home to New York from a recruiting presentation to undergraduates at Duke University (judging by the honking taxis, she was at the tail end of the trip). She described what she often sees in university students and millennials: "They want to know—'Am I working for an organization that has a sense of responsibility for making an impact to the communities more broadly?' So it's something we definitely talk about, and we talk about it because it's a reflection of the culture of the firm."

Does it come up more frequently in interviews than it did five or ten years ago? I asked. "I think it's always been on peoples' minds, but what happened is that candidates are far more direct in their questions about everything, including the organization's culture and philosophy. Their questions reflect their concerns of whether this an organization that reflects the purposes that matter to them. You know, the line between the value systems in their personal lives and the value systems of their professional life is blurred, and I think that's a very positive thing."

I made a note that she was telling a story very similar to that of Suzanne DiBianca at Salesforce. Her final words also reminded me of the macroperspective: "We believe that we're a better commercial enterprise for our clients and investors if we're aware of the significance of our voice and our involvement in things that matter to society. This also simply makes this a more interesting place to work."

The Goldman Sachs Gives Analyst Impact Fund is another proof point that layering in a sense of purpose does not mean you are breaking the bank. In this case, the money was already earmarked for deployment. But in a group brainstorm, the decision was made to allow the youngest employees to get involved and to make philanthropy a team sport. The teams had a bit of fun in an otherwise high-pressure environment. The motivational factor must have also been off the charts—one can only imagine how good it would feel as a young person to deliver such a significant amount of funding to a worthy cause you deeply believed in.

The Millennial Factor

The themes from the three examples above are amplified when you zero in on millennials—a new generation of employees who are requiring a new set of engagement policies. They're less motivated by the factors our parents considered when seeking employment, such as salary, job security, and pension plans.

We talked earlier in chapter 2 about how purpose can affect millennials' purchasing decisions and in chapter 3 about its impact on recruiting them, so it's no surprise that it also affects their motivation and retention levels at work.

According to a Cone Communications survey, more than two-thirds of millennials feel that their company's social and/or environmental activities make them feel proud to work there. This is not just the case in the United States, as shown by an Ernst & Young study of attitudes toward corruption in key Asian markets like China, Thailand, and Indonesia. While previous generations may have viewed corruption as a cost of doing business, the employees surveyed in 2015 did not take so sanguine an attitude. The Ernst & Young survey interviewed over fifteen hundred managers and employees in fourteen Asia-Pacific countries. Eight in ten respondents said that they would not work for an unethical firm. Among those under the age of twenty-five, the figure was nearly nine in ten employees.

Chris Fordham, a managing partner at Ernst & Young, told the South China Morning Post: "In Asia-Pacific, where the labor market is highly competitive, and it is already difficult to recruit and retain staff, the findings should be a wake-up call to businesses."

Purpose Knows No Age Limit

The Ernst & Young study shows that the desire to work in ethical and purpose-driven environments is not limited just to the young. It's also not exclusive to those who are highly educated. There's a classic behavioral study, conducted almost twenty years ago by the Yale organizational behavior professor Amy Wrzesniewski and colleagues, that focused on studying custodians in a major hospital. Though the custodians' official job duties didn't explicitly require them to interact with other people, many of them considered their work to include doing whatever they could to help ease the pain of patients and their families. They would try to make the patients laugh or calm them down and help family members find their way around. There was no financial incentive for the custodians to do this "extra" work, but they all said that it was this part of the job that made them want to get out of bed each morning. "I enjoy entertaining the patients," said one. "That's what I enjoy the most."

Having motivated employees is obviously a key to success for many companies. And once you've invested, and you have them, you've got to keep them. Gone are the days when a young person starting out in his or her career joined a company and automatically stayed until retirement. In today's business environment, there are no guarantees. Attrition has huge costs, never more so than when it's a high performer. Motivation is a first step that purpose can help with. Let's now turn to the flip side of that coin: retention.

You Could Lose the Whole Department

In the recruiting chapter, we heard from the Financial Times CEO John Ridding on the importance of purpose in recruiting the most sought-after employees. I once asked him if purpose also played a role in retention.

"Oh yes. When we know we may lose a key talent, we fight hard to keep them. And I lose sleep not just over that person because you know talent attracts talent, and depending on where that person goes, they could be a magnet that attracts other people. You don't just lose that person and their productivity—you could lose the whole department."

And many companies are doing just that. They may feel they've won the war for talent on the recruitment side but then lose it with attrition. Let's quickly geek out with some data from Life Work Solutions, a provider of staff-retention and consulting services. It shared the following turnover facts and rates:

- More than half of people recruited into an organization will leave within two years.
- One in four new hires will leave within six months.
- Nearly three-quarters of organizations report that staff turnover has a negative financial impact due to the cost of recruiting, hiring, and training a replacement employee and the overtime work of current employees.
- Nearly three-quarters of organizations report having difficulties in replacing staff.
- Approximately half of organizations experience regular problems with employee retention.

The ability to engage and retain valuable employees has a significant impact on an organization's bottom line. American businesses lose $11 billion annually because of employee turnover, according to the Bureau of National Affairs.

Part of the problem is that companies don't appreciate the impact of employee attrition until it's too late. Losing an employee isn't just a bummer. It's not simply a drain on the human resources department.

There are massive repercussions, and if managers understood the math more clearly, they wouldn't be so quick to patch up the problem of employee engagement with foosball and french fries.

Josh Bersin, founder of Bersin by Deloitte, outlined factors that a business should consider in calculating the "real" cost of losing an employee, including the cost of hiring a new employee, onboarding the employee, and the new employee's internal and customer-service errors, lost engagement, and lost productivity.

We should remember that people are what Bersin calls an "appreciating asset." His research has shown that "the longer we stay with an organization, the more productive we get—we learn the systems, we learn the products, and we learn how to work together."

According to the Studer Group, a Harvard Business School study of 610 CEOs estimated that the typical midlevel managers required 6.2 months to reach his or her break-even point. Bersin believes the job of top leadership and the HR team is "to attract the right people and move them up this curve as rapidly and effectively as possible."

The monetary cost is, of course, just the tip of the iceberg. We've all probably worked in environments where we experienced an "energy suck" when a highly talented superstar left our team or company. "Why?" people wonder. "Is there something wrong with us?"

How Companies Respond

As more companies realize that purpose can be a very cost-effective way to increase motivation and lower attrition, they've become much more strategic in how they set up their engagement programs. Many are abandoning the old lowest-common-denominator approach of having a single "day of service" in which they go out en masse to work in soup kitchens or clean up trash from the beach. I still recall one of my friends at a bank telling me how much he and his coworkers resented the annual top-down edict: "Why is painting park benches the best use of my time? There are many ways I can contribute that would have a higher value for charities that need my time, like helping them with their IT systems or cash-flow planning." A woman I met at a book-signing event complained about her firm: "It's the same thing every year—we're asked to put a Band-Aid on a problem, and we do it while all wearing T-shirts with our company logo and something on the back about us being a 'caring company.' And then, of course, we have the obligatory group photo that the firm will use for propaganda purposes."

Now I don't really hang out with cynical people, and yet I keep hearing similar complaints that many corporate initiatives feel like a one-off tactic rather than an actual strategy for the firm to make a real impact. "Does an annual day of service mean, the woman above asked, "that we're supposed to not be civic-minded the other 364 days of the year?"

Listening to this feedback, some companies are embracing the move toward skills-based volunteering programs. The idea is one that is simple and smart: rather than have a group of employees do unskilled labor for a day, a small number of them are given a more significant amount of time off (typically between two weeks and three months) to tackle a strategic problem in a way that takes advantage of their skills and talent. I first learned about this when Credit Suisse asked Room to Read to be part of the launch of their Global Citizens Program.

The program was piloted in 2010 and rolled out the following year with the goal of playing "matchmaker" between talented Credit Suisse employees and their international grant partners, including Accion, Plan International, Teach for All, and Women's World Banking. The partners identify a strategic project for which they do not have the required skill set or time internally, and the bank then identifies and recruits an employee with those skills. Like many great purpose-driven ideas, this one came from the front lines. Two employees managing the bank's newly launched global initiatives (the Microfinance Capacity-Building Initiative and the Global Education Initiative), Dawn Emling and Eva Halper, realized that there was an opportunity to go "beyond the check" and to support their partners through volunteering by sharing their relevant skills and experience honed in the business world.

They pitched the idea to two senior executives, who quickly signed on to have their own teams involved in a low-cost and rapid-to-implement pilot. Before long, human-resource executives were in Bangladesh and Ghana teaching about performance management to a rural hospital system, an expert on Salesforce was in Nepal teaching an education NGO how to move terabytes of education project data into the cloud, and data geeks were in Tanzania and Zambia helping microfinance organizations to better quantify their social impact.

Soon, the bank found that those who volunteered reported significantly higher levels of motivation and were much more likely to stay engaged in their jobs. An internal 2016 survey of those who had taken part in the program quantified many of the benefits:

- All felt proud that Credit Suisse was offering the opportunity to employees.
- Most were more likely to tell others (including potential customers and prospective employees) about the bank because of their experience.
- Almost all believed the program provided opportunities to develop and practice new skills in a way that wasn't offered through any formal training programs.
- Seven in ten identified their skilled volunteering experience as contributing to their decision to remain with the bank.
- Eight in ten felt more prepared to take on roles of increased responsibility at work and believed the experience had helped to improve their problem-solving skills.

One program participant was Aniket Patel, a London-based IT director whose volunteer assignment was with Teach for Argentina (Enseñá por Argentina). He took on the challenge of designing and running a training program to help senior staff members to increase their project management skills and to develop systems to monitor and control project progress. He shared his experience with me:

Taking part in the [program]...taught me so much about myself, the way in which I work, and the skills I have to offer, and these lessons continue to be relevant to me in my daily working life...It took me way outside my comfort zone and gave me the opportunity to apply my skills in an environment which is so different to daily life at Credit Suisse. It taught me more about how I work, what I know, what I have to offer to others, and how I can go about passing that knowledge on. It taught me not to underestimate myself, to be open, to take risks.

Credit Suisse executives I interviewed repeatedly talked about how it was not just the NGOs and volunteers who were benefitting but also the bank. It helped that volunteers learned about frontier markets, how NGOs manage to always "do more with less," what life is like for the unbanked, and the growth of the informal credit and banking sectors in less developed nations.

The program has become so popular that there is now a perpetual waiting list.

What is true at Credit Suisse has also been shown in other organizations with similar programs. Studies of skilled volunteering programs at companies including Microsoft, EY, GlaxoSmithKline, and others have found that 92 percent of participants recognized their experience had led to positive development in leadership skills and competencies.

Overruling Steve Jobs

For all his fame and fortune, Steve Jobs had what some consider to be a blight on his record: he notoriously pooh-poohed corporate philanthropy.

When asked why he had not, for example, joined other billionaires like Warren Buffett and Bill Gates in signing the Giving Pledge (promising to give away half your net worth to good causes), Jobs often claimed to be too busy or replied that it was through Apple's products that he could do the most good for humanity. He was criticized in the media, as reporters pointed out that many other CEOs and founders are also busy yet managed to hire and delegate to the right people, with the goal of getting funds out of the bank vault and onto the playing field of social change.

In 1997, when Jobs returned for his second stint as CEO, he shut down all the company's charity programs—shut them down!

Steve was a man of great charisma, and his presentations were undeniably entertaining, but many felt he sidestepped the responsibilities that come with great wealth and power. How was a company with annual profits exceeding $30 billion and a cash pile of over $250 billion able to justify never matching the $1,000 check that a hardworking employee might donate to breast-cancer research or the local dog shelter?

I had heard feedback from a disgruntled employee who had written a check to Room to Read. When we asked if he could double his commitment by applying for corporate matching, he sheepishly admitted that he could not. "Quite frankly, it's embarrassing. Here we are, one of the three most valuable companies in the world, and we're too cheap to do what every other company considers to be the baseline standard."

Not a lot of people get to overrule a leader like Steve Jobs. But after his death, the mantle of CEO was passed to Tim Cook, who seems to recognize the role that purpose plays in motivating and retaining the troops. Within a month of becoming CEO, Cook announced that a corporate matching program would be launched immediately, with a very generous ceiling of $10,000 per employee.

The above stories point out that purpose is often a journey, not a destination. Strategies will indeed migrate over time. We may not always get it right, but that doesn't mean we should stop trying.

And you can always assure yourselves that even if you mess it up, there is no way in the world you could screw it up as badly as Larry Ellison did. And with that, please allow me to now tell you the story of one of the most expensive attritions in the history of modern capitalism.

The Cost of This Lost Employee: $60 Billion

When we talk about the high cost of attrition, one of my favorite examples to cite comes courtesy of software giant Oracle. During my days at Microsoft, we often talked about "Where would you be working if you weren't here?" The company that almost never came up was the behemoth founded by Larry Ellison. It was widely considered to be a grind or the machine, which would take everything it could get from you before unceremoniously spitting you out. Their pay packages could be legendary, especially for the best salespeople, and as a result, the company mostly attracted the most mercenary people—those willing to sell their souls for a few extra gold coins.

One key executive who apparently agreed with this consensus was the founder of a company we profiled in the last chapter: Salesforce's Marc Benioff. Marc started his career at Oracle, rose rapidly through the ranks, and was once one of Larry Ellison's most trusted lieutenants. But then one day, at the top of his game, he chose to walk.

Marc had an idea to build a business around the then-radical notion that a company's entire IT infrastructure should reside "in the cloud." It seemed every bit as ethereal then as the name implied, especially in the era prior to speedy and ubiquitous Internet connections. He pursued this passion with laserlike focus, even going so far as to choose the ticker symbol CRM (customer-relationship management was the young company's initial area of focus) when the company went public.

Given that Oracle was the king of database-management software and had billions of dollars on its balance sheet, why did Benioff choose to start the company outside of Oracle? Lots of companies encourage their stars to be "intrapreneurs" ("employees who are assigned a special idea or project and are instructed to develop it as an entrepreneur would").

Marc most certainly had Ellison's trust and could likely have negotiated a highly motivating incentive package if his new idea turned into a significant source of funding for Oracle. So why did he choose to strike out on his own?

"It came out of my discontent. At Oracle everything was institutionalized, and no one cared. We wanted something more connected, something that had more community."

During his 2015 commencement speech at UC Berkeley, Benioff talked about his first full-time job at Oracle, and how after thirteen years at the company, he realized it wasn't enough. "I felt strongly in my heart there must be more to the values of business than what I was experiencing at Oracle. I came to the realization that companies can do much more than build and sell products. They can be a platform for change. They can tap into much higher values. And they can improve the state of the world. So when I started my company in 1999, I made a commitment to this vision."

He confessed in an interview with *Fast Company*:

When I was at Oracle, I felt deep inside myself that there was this bifurcation. I was working for this company, and that was one way of life, and there was another way of life that was the nonprofit world or spiritual world, whatever you want to call it. I went on this tour of India in 1996, talking to gurus, incense wafting over us, and suddenly it became clear to me that there was a way to integrate all of this—that you could do both at the same time. Why do I have to be two people? Can't I just be one person? I want to live an integrated life. I want to be an integrated leader.

So he left, and upon launching his startup, he integrated many components he'd found missing at Oracle, such as the one-one-one pledge and the paid time off for volunteering outlined in the prior chapter.

Salesforce has recruited over twenty-six thousand highly motivated employees since its founding in 2000, and keep in mind, it's been trying to win the war for talent in the white-hot San Francisco and Silicon Valley markets. Company executives say that a strong sense of purpose is key not just to recruiting but also to keeping their people highly motivated. In the previous chapter, SVP of philanthropy Suzanne DiBianca talked about millennial employees' "very blurred line between work and life" and their desire to "bring their whole selves to work," with an employer who is a good corporate citizen. Is it working? Let's run the numbers:

- A recent Salesforce employee survey found that 96 percent "feel good about the way [the company] contributes to the community."
- Under their theme of "winning as a team," 94 percent of employees say people are willing to give extra to get the job done.
- With the goal of "rallying together as a family," 92 percent of employees agree that "people care about each other here."

Salesforce was named one of the world's most innovative companies by Forbes six years in a row. The company has made Fortune's annual list of the one hundred best places to work for nine consecutive years. Its most recent ranking: number eight.

The result? Internal surveys show that an incredible 96 percent of employees are proud to tell others they work at Salesforce. And that's a number you can take to the bank, because when your employees are that motivated, you're not losing many of them. And for Salesforce, which has always enjoyed rapid growth, that employee buzz is a heck of a lot cheaper than hiring search firms.

In essence, Marc left his old role so that someday his employees wouldn't have to.

Closing Thoughts

Having a strong sense of purpose is no guarantee that you will always have motivated employees who stick around. You still must look out for their other needs and desires. But connecting them to a cause that's higher than just this quarter's revenues or earnings per share can be one strong step in the right direction. As Edwards Lifesciences CEO Mike Mussallem told me when I asked him about retaining a fired-up workforce, "Having purpose does not guarantee you'll have a great company. But lack of a purpose is enough to guarantee that you won't be great."

And with that, let's now turn our attention to how purpose can not only motivate employees but also connect people who may sit outside your organization but are nonetheless critical to its success. It turns out that purpose can also connect entire supply chains and business ecosystems.

6

Purpose and Partnerships: Unifying Your Ecosystem

Purpose can be a powerful way to unite coworkers behind a common cause, but it doesn't have to stop with those who are on the same payroll. Some of our smartest companies are finding that purpose can reach far beyond a company's walls to unite their entire supply chain.

Supply chains and business ecosystems mattered a lot less in the old days. (Because *ecosystem* is the more all-encompassing of the two phrases, I use only that term going forward.) Companies typically owned and directly controlled most of their means of production. Vertical integration, in which a business set up complete control over a product's production—from raw materials to final assembly—was the order of the day. Few companies provide better examples of that bygone era than Ford, with its River Rouge plant, constructed from 1917 until 1928. The facility was one mile long and one and a half miles wide and included ninety-three buildings with sixteen million feet of factory floor space. To put its size in perspective, there were over one hundred miles of internal railroad tracks, and the plant employed over one hundred thousand workers at its peak. Given that the factory contained everything from its own energy plant to an integrated steel mill, the titanic Rouge plant was able to transform raw materials into running vehicles within a single complex. Iron ore and coke roll in; Model Ts roll out!

They say no man is an island, but in the old days, many companies clearly were. Yes, Ford had to negotiate with suppliers, but these were typical for low-margin commodities like carbon, oil, glass, and rubber, with decisions often coming down to pure cost considerations. Today's most successful businesses, by contrast, pursue strategies that are much more asset-light. Apple does not design or manufacture its own chips—it relies on suppliers like Broadcomm, Cirrus Logic, Qualcomm, and Texas Instruments. It sources its ultrathin glass screens from Corning, LG, and Samsung. Sony and Omnivision provide the cameras. In many cases, it doesn't even assemble the final product—Foxconn does the assembly for all iPhones in China and then ships the product to intermediate warehouses owned by UPS and FedEx. This is, in short, anything but River Rouge—and the significantly lower asset base means that each dollar of profit (and boy, do they make profits!) results in a much higher return on net assets.

Ford in the 1930s versus Apple may be an extreme comparison, but it's a good starting point to show how the model has shifted, with many companies today pursuing asset-light models. Employee-light too! I still remember how surprised I was when I joined Microsoft to learn how many of the people around me weren't on the payroll. From the guys cutting the lawn to the receptionists, from the friendly guy serving pizza in the cafeteria to the workers boxing the software, they were not on our own payroll but rather that of suppliers.

All around us today, we see companies pursuing similar asset-light strategies. As they do, the success of a company becomes more heavily dependent upon its ecosystem. Whole Foods and Trader Joe's work with many hundreds of suppliers to stock those shelves with free-range eggs, organic yogurt, and peanut-butter pretzels.

The Four Seasons can't tap into growing travel markets such as China, India, and Indonesia (that's 2.9 billion potential customers right there) unless it works closely with the largest online travel agents in each market. BMW will not have the latest navigation and safety technology unless it's tied to cutting-edge firms from Pittsburgh to Munich. The major ride-sharing companies—Uber and Lyft in the United States, Didi in China, and Ola Cabs in India—pursue an asset-light model where they don't own the actual cars; they're therefore completely dependent upon their drivers. Tatcha can't sell its products without retail distribution partners like Barneys, QVC, and Sephora. Finally, Starbucks in the United States and Caffè Nero in the UK are working closely with coffee suppliers in locations ranging from Guatemala to Tanzania, tea farms in India and Sri Lanka, and local suppliers of everything ranging from cups to sugar to milk. The list goes on, but I won't.

Businesses are exposed to more risks as they continue to become more reliant on their ecosystems. When vertical integration was common, everyone reported up the same chain of command. Now, there are multiple organizations with multiple bosses, and in many cases, your suppliers might also be working with your competitors. There's always a risk of "us versus them," of "insiders versus outsiders," of every business problem ranging from silos to suspicion to lack of communications.

In his book *Uncommon Sense, Common Nonsense*, the writer Jules Goddard argues:

> In the near future, companies may no longer be able to rely on imposed employment contracts and internal organizational structures to get work

done. They will need to reach out to extended networks of gifted freelancers and find creative ways of engaging their talents if they are to remain competitive. *On their own, companies will simply not have access to sufficient talent to innovate and survive.* The critical competence of organizations will become their ability to earn their membership of highly creative networks critical to their own success—by contributing at least as much value to these communities as they receive. (emphasis mine)

Does it sound like your job just got a little bit harder? Yes, it did! You are or will be challenged to work closely and in unison not just with your coworkers but with hundreds of people you've not yet even met and over whom you don't have the formal power that comes with old-style employment contracts.

Can purpose play a role in building out and motivating that network? I think it can and should. But it's a challenge.

Dr. Diane Mollenkopf, the McCormick Associate Professor of Logistics at the Haslam College of Business, University of Tennessee, recalls focus groups she has conducted in the past decade about sustainability. "We'd get people talking about the 'green' initiatives at their companies, and we'd get lots of excited responses about the company's 'green' initiatives (things like printing double sided instead of single sided, energy-efficient lighting in offices, etc.)…then we'd ask specifically about their 'green supply-chain initiatives' and the room invariably grew silent."

There are success stories, though. Let's start small, with a company you've likely never heard of, in an industry you might consider quite old-school, and take a short journey to Surrey, British Columbia.

It's Always Good to Talk about Something other than Prices

Raven Hydronic Supply works with old-line industrial products you might consider to be unglamorous. Ever talked at a cocktail party about boilers, water heaters, and coils? No? How about flex connectors, pumps, and storage tanks? I love—and start with—the Raven example because it tells the story of how any company in any industry can unite its ecosystem with a well-designed and purpose-driven strategy.

I first heard of Raven when one of their employees, Ashley Bouchard, contacted the Room to Read chapter leaders in nearby Vancouver. She had suggested to the firm's president, Brian DeJaegher, that the company should take on a new charity initiative and then asked our team for a list of projects that needed funding. A school-construction project in Nepal was chosen, and what would become a unique annual campaign was kicked off.

Bouchard's idea was that instead of funding the project all by themselves, they'd ask their suppliers to get involved as well. The goal was to unite their entire ecosystem in a common cause. Why have all the fun alone when you can instead involve the companies with whom you work on a day-to-day basis?

Bouchard and DeJaegher designed a creative and inclusive strategy:

- "To prove that we had skin in the game," Raven would match all donations from suppliers on a one-to-one basis.
- Recognizing that most suppliers likely did not have charitable budgets, they did not ask for a straight-up donation. Instead, they asked each supplier to give a discount on the next invoice they sent to Raven. If they were billing Raven for $10,000, then perhaps they could offer a 2 percent discount, pitching in $200 that would be matched by Raven and get the team $400 closer to the goal.
- The team was taught to sell the program effectively by reminding each supplier that "we're not asking for ourselves; we're asking so that kids in Nepal can have a new school." Bouchard told me, "We figured since we were asking for a discount to help educate children, it would be pretty hard to say no."
- Finally, the team let its vendors know that this was not

something it would be doing on a regular basis. It might do the program on an annual basis, but the vendor could rest assured that it would only be asked to knock 2 percent off a single invoice once a year.

The campaign got off to a charmed start. DeJaegher lit up with a wide smile as he reported that "the very first vendor we approached had vacationed in Nepal, so it was an easy first sell. He has become one of the strongest supporters of the program." Most of the company's vendors—including trucking firms, its communications suppliers, and anyone else who would listen to the pitch—gave the same answer.

Bouchard and DeJaegher later told me about the business benefits of the campaign:

- The unified team of employees plus vendors felt united in a quest that would do some good for the world. British Columbia is a very diverse province, and the campaign helped to connect people across many ethnicities and religions. "Our vendors were so excited to join in, and it was great for our employees because it gave us something really positive to talk with our vendors about, whether it was in a meeting or on the phone."
- Brian relayed that they "would bring it up during sales calls and found that it was always good to find a way to talk about something other than products and price." Ashley added: "We grew our relationships on a whole other level. Instead of just talking about business, we talked about our own involvement with other charities, volunteering, our kids and families, etc. It helped to change and improve the usual conversation because it gave us a bigger picture topic that excited us."
- Much to the team's surprise, several customers got in touch to inquire, "Why aren't you also asking us for money? We'd like to be involved also." It turned out that so many of Raven's people were talking about the campaign that customers heard

about it too and wanted to join in the shared quest. The Raven team replied that "we already have line of sight to getting the school funded, so how about if our customers fund a library?" An additional part of its ecosystem was soon part of the team.

- Finally, the conversation was ongoing, as raising the funding was only the first part. As the schoolrooms were constructed and as the library was implemented, Ashley sent out updates to the entire ecosystem. "Because we send them regular updates and photos, it's always the topic of conversation."

Raven is an ideal purpose success story, as it shows that purpose can unite an ecosystem whether it be large or small. The idea need not be overly complex, and if it works well, it can become a sustained (or annual) campaign. Ashley summed it all up quite well: "It created this intangible bond that made us all feel this sense of union."

The bottom line is this: purpose connects, and connections are good for business.

This is even truer when connections *are* your business, as is the case for a company you no doubt have heard of and likely encounter several times a day.

Google Built It, but They Didn't Come

Ezekiel Vidra had a big challenge on his hands. The thirty-seven-year-old Israeli was recruited by Google in 2011 to launch one of its new initiatives: Campus London. The company's goal was to create a shared space where the European start-up community could come together to work, share ideas, brainstorm, and learn from a series of visiting speakers. Their pitch: "Rather than working out of coffeehouses or your parents' basement, work out of Campus London." The "campus" was a seven-story building Google acquired in the Shoreditch neighborhood. Entrepreneurs were invited to "Come start something," with the promise that Campus London would offer "Strong community to show you the way. Strong coffee to start the journey."

Membership was free, as was the Wi-Fi—*so what was in it for Google?* Their goal—and Vidra's challenge—was to help unify a sprawling and previously unconnected ecosystem of hundreds of technology start-ups and in so doing, gain an "early look" at companies that could become part of Google's ecosystem. They hoped, for example, that application developers would optimize for the Android platform, while also building in interoperability with Google's search engine, mapping, and alerts. Companies might get hooked on Google's email system, online word processing, and spreadsheets. Some might even have potential as investee companies for Google's venture-capital arm, as Google Ventures was a "second hat" worn by Vidra.

The hope was to quickly scale up a successful pilot and then expand to other cities, including Madrid, São Paulo, Seoul, Tel Aviv, and Warsaw.

The early months were not promising. Google built it, but they didn't come.

Vidra identified two issues that were impeding early success. First, many start-ups are suspicious when assessing the motivations of other tech companies—especially when they're behemoths like Google. "Are we going after the same customers?" "Are we chasing the same investors?" "How do I know they won't try to steal our IP or poach our best employees?" "Is there a risk that this free Wi-Fi will, in the end, turn out to be a bad bargain?"

The second issue was that those companies that were coming to campus weren't interacting with each other. The promise of "community" and "shared best practices" didn't hold much weight if everyone was failing to collect his or her prize. Vidra told me, "Some people were hanging out, but they weren't engaging. They were staring at their screens rather than talking to each other. Granted, we techies have a reputation as being introverted geeks who will send an instant message to the person sitting across the table rather than actually talking to them," he said with a laugh, "but this was extreme, and as our newly minted head of campus, it was my job to fix it."

Meet London's Newest Start-Up

One day during his morning commute, Vidra was pondering the issue: "How do I get the start-up community to come together in an environment of mutual trust?" And then the synapses fired. He'd noted that London's commuter cycling lanes were increasingly crowded, especially among young tech workers. Why not, he thought, invite the tech community to come together around a new challenge—a multiday group charity ride? "If I can get everyone to focus on a shared cause, then it gives us a safe, neutral space to unite. People will drop their guard and hopefully also their introverted natures. And since education has played such a critical role in all our lives, I decided that each rider would be asked to raise a minimum of £1,000 for Room to Read."

With the slogan "Put down your laptops and pick up your bikes," the newest start-up in London—TechBikers—was born. The pitch to riders: You'd leave London's St. Pancras station on Thursday's 5:00 p.m. Eurostar. Arrive in Paris by 8:00 p.m., enjoy a carbohydrate-rich dinner and a good night's sleep, and then the next day, point that bike north and begin riding the 320 kilometers back to London. Your friends, family, and coworkers would be waiting at the finish line in Shoreditch on Sunday afternoon with cold beer, food, and hopefully some Bengay for those tired joints.

Vidra, a gregarious sales guy, went to work immediately. "That very day," he told me, "I created an online post titled 'Crazy Idea,' asking who would be interested in joining me on a ride from Paris to London. When fifty people signed up their interest within forty-eight hours, I knew I was onto something. I had no website, no logo, no logistics company to manage the ride. But if there's a will, there's a way!"

Under the theory of "don't let the perfect be the enemy of the good," Vidra set four simple goals for the initial ride: (1) recruit a bike touring company to whom he could outsource logistics, (2) convince companies to underwrite the event costs (support vehicles, mechanics, and meals) so that all funds raised could go directly to charity, (3) bring everyone home safely, and (4) make sure the cyclists had such a good time that they'd commit to making it an annual event.

Just three months later, the Eurostar train departed St. Pancras with seventy bikes and seventy eager TechBikers on board! Next stop—Gare du Nord!

Rains of Biblical Proportions

Paris, Friday morning. The weather is perfect for a group photo under the Eiffel Tower. Many are in awe that one TechBiker is doing the entire ride on a clunky London ride-share bike—the kind designed for short rides. Others are laughing at Vidra: "Since I was so busy with the launch of Google's Campus," Vidra said, "I didn't have any time to train at all. When we got to Paris, it was literally my first time on a road bike. I was asking people how exactly you shift the gears, and they laughed at me since I was pointing at the brake. Still, others are taking photos with an unlikely participant in the ride: a sixty-year-old blind man."

As the group rode north, people meeting for the first time bonded over photo ops, fixing of flats, and the sharing of energy bars and sunscreen. Their spirits were only slightly dampened by the forecast for rains "of biblical proportions" in both the north of France and the south of England.

Three days later, a wet and exhausted peloton crossed the finish line in Shoreditch. As beer bottles clinked over finish-line toasts, Vidra smiled as he was repeatedly asked, "Same time next year?"

Unifying the Tech Community

Six years on, the TechBiker movement continues to grow. Over four hundred riders have taken part in the Paris-to-London ride, raising over $600,000 to support education projects around the world. Other

European techies catalyzed new multiday charity rides, including Vienna to Budapest and Copenhagen to Berlin, allowing more connections between techies across geographies.

According to Eze, Google measured the success, or impact, of Campus according to the following metrics: by building community, promoting diversity (Campus has a much higher female participation than the standard tech-industry hub, at 34 percent—"Still work left to do!"), funding raised by the start-ups at Campus, and jobs created.

Vidra says that second only to a large amount of funding raised for education, he's most proud of having brought together so many people who might not otherwise have met: "You can meet people at events or over drinks many times," he said, "and you will rarely make a real connection. But cycle with them for three days, and you make friends for life. The camaraderie that takes place on the road extends beyond the road to our professional lives. We meet for reunions, training rides, and even have online TechBikers alumni chat groups on both WhatsApp and Facebook." Several entrepreneurs who met through TechBikers became cofounders of new companies, and many others found their next gig.

A week before the Paris-to-London cycle, Jillian Kowalchuk got a call from her friend Megan, who was registered for the ride but had gotten herself into a minor cycling accident and was hoping Jillian would take her place.

"Hearing how touched she was by Room to Read and what a once-in-a-lifetime opportunity it would be, I felt the surge of adrenaline and my little voice in my head saying, 'Are you crazy?' right before I agreed," says Jillian. "The online research I did for Room to Read was exactly aligned with personal and business passions to empower women. Founding the mobile app Safe & The City, which creates personalized walking routes to avoid sexual harassment and aggression, I recognize how vital education and safe places are to empower the next generation of women."

Jillian was welcomed into the TechBikers WhatsApp group and cheered for her commitment to do the ride and continue the fundraising efforts. "In the few short weeks after, I have noticed a profound difference this group had on me personally and professionally. As an early-stage solo founder, there is an enormous amount of weight and pressure, especially when building a team and product while trying to raise finance. The group dynamics allowed me to meet brilliant VCs, developers, and other entrepreneurs who could swap stories, find ways to help one another, or give another nudge of encouragement to keep going. One fellow TechBiker even offered his support to act as my CTO to support our continued development after a challenging time. The TechBiker community is one that pushes me, shows me there are wonderful people who can also be wildly successful, and gives me the opportunity to launch myself and my business to the next level."

And then there's Toby Sims. "I was quite new to the London tech scene, having retrained as a web developer from a career in grantsmanship with the General Assembly and found the openness of tech meet-ups and the 'how can I help?' ethos very comforting in a quite interesting time. I'd started to hear about TechBikers through mutual in-person and social-media friends and thought, why not?

"By the time I had signed up for TechBikers, I'd got good links in the tech scene and made some good friends but might have been accused of 'running in the same circles.' TechBikers introduced me to a lot of new faces I wouldn't have necessarily met for a while, due to my heavy developer focus.

"Whilst on the ride, I got chatting to a fellow biker and the usual 'so what is it you do?' conversation came about over some gentle inclines, and he responded, 'I work for a little start-up called Shaken Cocktails.' Six months later, I agreed to a new job on the strength of a signature on a napkin at a very inappropriate time in the morning after a very fine selection of spirits."

Vidra summarizes it best: "TechBikers has become one of the biggest unifying events among the London start-up community, and we're seen as the catalyst and convener. We're such a big company, and I think we seem less scary when we're doing good for the world. It's also been great for building my own network—I've now met and bonded with hundreds of people who might have otherwise remained strangers."

Purpose: A Hurricane Force

As a recent promotional video for Airbnb put it: "We're more than just a website. We're an opportunity to connect to people, to places, to neighborhoods, in a whole new way."

Airbnb was not the first home-sharing site, and it was challenged not only by incumbents like HomeAway and One Fine Stay but also by copycats like Wimdu in Germany. To its idealistic cofounders, one of the main differentiating features of Airbnb would always be its sense of mission (to help create "a world where you can belong anywhere and where people can live a place, instead of just traveling to it"[33]) and "the way it cultivated an intimate community among its users."[34]

Like Ashley Bouchard at Raven, Airbnb found ways to use purpose to unify its ecosystem—in this case, one that spans the globe. In Airbnb's case, it was really something that it stumbled upon. Like many purpose-driven initiatives, Airbnb's bubbled up democratically from the site's members, with the corporate team being savvy enough to quickly pattern-match and replicate the program across many key markets.

When Hurricane Sandy slammed into the east coast of the United States in October 2012, it quickly became the second most destructive storm ever to hit the United States at that time. Over 250 people were killed, and the damage amounted to over $75 billion. Seven point nine million homes and businesses lost power, and thousands of flights were canceled at dozens of airports up and down the East Coast. A thirteen-foot wall of water hit lower Manhattan, resulting in the first two-day shutdown of the New York Stock Exchange since 1888. With hurricane winds reaching 175 miles per hour, nearly every form of transportation, including buses, trains, and subways, was shut down, stranding tens of thousands of people in unfamiliar locations.

Into the situation stepped a woman named Shell. A real-estate professional of Puerto Rican descent, she was a long-time Airbnb host who realized that many people had lost their homes, while others were travelers stranded by the transportation shutdown. "A sinking feeling hit my stomach as I thought, people are going to get stuck."

She decided to go online and list her property as being available at no cost to anyone stranded or made homeless by the storm. Other hosts heard about her initiative, and within days over four hundred people had emulated her example, offering "not only a place to sleep but a warm connection during a very uncertain time."[35]

Shell believed that offering her home for free was one of the best decisions she ever made. "Sometimes people don't connect that much in New York, and you can feel isolated. Inviting guests in during Hurricane Sandy brought a sense of community right into my home."[36] She did not stop there; she also launched a community food drive run out of her kitchen to help those in need.

From Little Things, Big Things Grow

Shell likely did not know how big a difference her decision would make. Proving that imitation is the sincerest form of flattery, the Airbnb team decided to institutionalize and formalize a new disaster-response initiative. The company hired Kellie Bentz for the newly created position of head of global disaster relief. Bentz had worked in New Orleans in the aftermath of Hurricane Katrina, where she started a disaster-recovery program called HandsOn New Orleans. The program had provided housing for volunteers, assembled crews to help with the rebuilding of homes, and partnered with companies to rebuild schools, public parks, and community centers. She later worked as the senior director of disaster services for Points of Light, the largest volunteer network in the world, where she led volunteer responses to numerous disasters, including the Japanese tsunami and earthquake in 2011.

Bentz liked the idea of allowing Airbnb hosts to quickly volunteer to be part of the solution. "Throughout my career, I've seen the terrible devastation that disasters can inflict, but I've also seen the powerful ways that communities come together to respond and recover...We have a real opportunity to use our disaster response program to help these communities in a time of need."[37]

The impact has been felt around the world, with hosts offering free lodging in forty-seven emergency situations to date, including the 2015 earthquakes in both Japan and Nepal. Because the company had formalized its relationship with government agencies like the US Federal Emergency Management Agency (FEMA) and volunteer-focused nonprofits like All Hands, it could quickly mobilize. Erik Dyson, the CEO of All Hands, reported on the symbiotic relationship with Airbnb during the aftermath of the two devastating earthquakes that hit Nepal, killing over nine thousand people:

Airbnb's ability to quickly find local hosts that were willing to contribute their space, free of charge, allowed [us] to overcome one of the biggest challenges we face in responding to a natural disaster: finding a safe place for the team and volunteers to stay. This meant we were on the ground working in a matter of days after the Nepal earthquake. This flexibility is crucial to our success.[38]

The program has continued to grow and is no longer limited to natural disasters; it also responds to man-made ones. When US president Donald Trump unexpectedly sprang his Muslim travel ban on the world in December 2016, it affected thousands of travelers, including a Yemeni refugee named Zak. Zak had landed in Denver one day before the travel ban was issued. He was fortunate to have arrived, but the other refugees with whom he had planned to room were barred from entry into the United States.

The International Rescue Committee, also an Airbnb partner, reached out to a Denver couple named Susan and Steve to ask if they could temporarily house Zak. They immediately said yes and quickly bonded with Zak. Not content to stop at simply offering housing, they soon enlisted the help of friends, family, and neighbors to help Zak find a part-time job and permanent, long-term housing. "When we agreed to house Zak, we didn't know how special the meaning of that 'yes' would be. Zak is a joyful and beautiful person. He's interested in every dimension of life, people, and the arts—we consider him a close friend."[39]

Susan and Steve did not stop there. Their home became a regular "point of landing" for refugees from the Middle East, a reflection of what they called the community spirit of the city of Denver. Airbnb formalized its commitment to the program, publicly announcing a goal of providing "short-term housing over the next five years for 100,000 people in need, starting with refugees, disaster survivors, and relief workers." They also made a $4 million commitment to the International Rescue Committee.

In Airbnb's case, a desire to optimize the supply chain for purpose led to a bump in profit, but there are corporate examples when it goes in the opposite direction, and a desire to optimize the supply chain for *profit* leads the decision makers to *purpose*.

Not So Fast...

So, it's settled then? I've listed several successful, high-profile deployments of purpose, and the world is probably following suit as I type this, right? We all know it's never that simple. In 2010, when Accenture surveyed more than seven hundred members of the United Nations Global Compact on sustainable business practices, 96 percent of CEOs told us that sustainability should be integrated into all aspects of strategy and operations, yet only 54 percent of those CEOs affirmed that they had achieved supply-chain sustainability.

The truth is that ecosystems are not the easiest ships to course-correct.

Even if you as a company have high sustainability standards, issues of visibility and oversight might run you into challenges with enforcement.

When Apple produced a progress report on its supplier responsibility in 2012, the company discovered that almost two-thirds of its suppliers did not comply with its stated factory limit of sixty hours per week. Also, more than a third of Apple's suppliers failed to meet its workplace-safety standards, while nearly a third did not comply with the company's hazmat-management practices.

When it comes to enforcement, companies need to think outside the box. For a bit of inspiration, look to the General.

The General Goes Green

General Motors turned to purpose to address concerns around the scarcity of future natural resources and the impact on its supply chain. It was the World Wildlife Fund who first drew the company's attention to the negative impact that farming natural rubber can have on the environment and its contributions to deforestation in Southeast Asia.

"We work with more than eighteen thousand suppliers around the world, and they, in turn, work with thousands of other suppliers. When you stop to consider their collective impact starting at the raw-material level, it's staggering, even now, after so much progress has already been made. Our multitiered supply chain produces ten times the greenhouse gas emissions of our facilities."

As a result, GM became the first automaker to commit to sourcing sustainable natural rubber in its tires and announced a goal of net-zero deforestation.

The company believes reducing the carbon footprint of its supply chain has many community, business, and environmental benefits, including these:

- Preserving and restoring primary forests and high-conservation-value and high-carbon-stock areas that are critical to addressing climate change and protecting wildlife
- Improving yield and quality for natural-rubber farmers, further supporting the small businesses that contribute 85 percent of this material
- Mitigating business risk related to supply-chain sourcing and performance and helping assure long-term availability of a key commodity

If carbon emissions can be reduced through optimization and greater efficiencies, costs go down, and that makes business sense.

But GM's senior VP of global purchasing and supply chain, Steve Kiefer, knows the dangers of lip service, even quoting the great American essayist Ralph Waldo Emerson: "What you do speaks so loud that I cannot hear what you say."

"General Motors expects a lot of the partners participating in its vast supply chain, and to help them understand its vision, the company needs actions that are louder than our words."

To further demonstrate its commitment, GM has recently announced that it will source all electrical power for its 350 facilities in fifty-nine countries with renewable energy by 2050. Kiefer is proud to add that "We are the only automaker to make such a commitment with a target completion date."

GM also outlined its expectations for supplier conduct in both its purchase contract terms and conditions, as well as in its new Supplier Code of Conduct, which the company rolled out to its entire supply base last month.

Kiefer says, "Our goal is also to be a zero-waste manufacturer, a commitment that has led to our having 152 landfill-free facilities around the world. GM is also developing a set of purchasing requirements intended to accelerate progress already made and address the barriers that remain, such as the traceability of rubber from farm to factory, and assurance of responsible practices used to produce it."

At the same time, GM is taking actions that can help achieve the same goals well known from do-gooding global nonprofits such as the Sierra Club and the Natural Resource Defense Council—those of reducing deforestation and habitat loss. Can you imagine the benefits of having major nonprofit experts and business-sharing practices and insight?

"We asked about two hundred of our suppliers to disclose their energy use and carbon-emission data to CDP and offered to share our best practices and our resources to help. About 70 percent of the invited companies responded, and CDP reported that they had reduced total carbon emissions by a collective ninety million metric tons, saving a cumulative $23 billion. Think about that…$23 billion, for only about 140 different companies. That really shows you the impact this has, both in terms of collective carbon footprint and collective financial results."

GM has identified four areas of opportunity to create a more sustainable supply chain. They include (1) harmonizing requirements for suppliers industry-wide so these companies aren't burdened by different requirements for similar sustainability data and information; (2) engaging the entire supply chain (not just the first tier of suppliers but engineering sustainable practices from first supplier to last); (3) using fact-based positive messages about how sustainability efforts can drive efficiency, savings, innovation, and risk; and (4) creating partnerships and collaborations that bring ideas and people together to fuel the movement.

"Through these partnerships and many others, we can champion and facilitate better performance all around," Kiefer said. "This means more energy efficiency, lower carbon intensity, fewer miles traveled— all of which saves money. What's the end game? When aggregated up the value chain, that means a more affordable product for our customers and lower costs to own and operate our vehicles."

Incorporating sustainability into your ecosystem is complicated, but a failure to do so may be the biggest risk of all.

Closing Thoughts

The beauty of purpose, when it comes to improving the health of your ecosystem, is that it has the power to make you feel like you're all on the same team. Sure, you could argue that a company and its suppliers have goals in common to begin with, but these partnerships are usually characterized by contractual goals drafted by lawyers, without any informal ones that come from the heart. They can often feel competitive, resembling a never-ending negotiation, with you and your suppliers on opposite sides of the table.

In the face of this, finding a common social good to rally around can remind you of each other's humanity. It will remind you that you share more than just a bottom line but also this planet. You'll be more willing and able to talk about subjects beyond the day's business and will find it makes you more sympathetic, more generous, more forgiving, more *chill*—all of which can help your ecosystem run more smoothly.

7

Attract the Best Investors

(*Psst.* This is a chapter about investors. You may not think you have to care about investors. If, for example, you work for a big company, it's unlikely you think much about acquiring capital and maintaining investor relations—"Hey, that's not my department!" But I believe there's a powerful incentive to read this chapter regardless—so that you know more about where your next competitor is likely coming from. Plus, the right "headline investor" has a halo effect that can affect everything: employee recruitment, market perception, and even the company's valuation. And odds are, at least one of those elements *does* concern you.)

In the old days, entrepreneurs were often starved for capital. The big businesses with which they hoped to compete had many sizable advantages, with one of the biggest being that they had relatively easy access to capital, thanks to their long-term banking relationships. They could also turn to the public debt and equity markets. The fledgling entrepreneur would often wait days on end to get an appointment with a banker, only to learn that he or she was stodgy, snobby, and risk averse.

How times change! As of 2017, the world is awash in liquidity, with literally trillions of dollars sitting on the sidelines. In a low-to-negative interest-rate environment, investors can't get much return through the traditional holdings like bonds and bank deposits, so they're lining up to purchase equity in the most promising businesses.

By every measure, 2016 was an extremely busy year for venture capital, with the total amount of capital invested reaching its highest level since 2000. Over the course of twelve months, three hundred thousand angel investors invested \$21.3 billion, spread out over 64,380 deals.[40] Meanwhile, venture-capital firms invested even more—\$29.6 billion, spread out over 4,050 deals.

Of course, the natural follow-up question is, um, *how?* How did all those businesses swing it? How did they convince investors that theirs was a risk worth taking? A horse worth betting on?

Any successful business owner or chatty investor will tell you he or she looks for some combination of the following: a good team, a great business plan, a solid exit strategy, conservative financial projections, and domain expertise. Another investor friend says, "You want your affairs to be in order. You want to be honest. You want to know your competition."

These are important, but they're also obvious. These are the qualities you need to be a contender, but what gets you the championship belt?

I'll let you in on a little secret: the unique differentiator isn't financial. It's not always a function of x sum of money being greater than y sum of money, because investors are more than just ATMs, and if you watch enough *Shark Tank* episodes, you know that there's more to a good deal than cash and terms.

It often comes down to passion. And I believe that passion often comes down to purpose.

Right now, you probably believe that investors don't care about that stuff—that they are even, ostensibly, the people who would care *least* about it. An investor's job is literally *all* about making moolah and financial returns, so how can the "pursuit of purpose" not sound like a horrible distraction to him or her?

Now, don't get me wrong. I'm not telling you to walk into investor meetings and lecture them on the importance of digging water wells in Africa. This isn't about a bait and switch or tacking on a phony CSR component for show. But I know, based on my own experience and my conversations with many investors, that your odds of securing funding increase if you can answer the question, "Why does your work *matter?*"

But don't take my word for it. Here's one of the most preeminent investors of our day: Chris Sacca.

The View from the Shark Tank

Many hundreds of start-ups would love to have Chris Sacca as an early investor. Sacca is best known as a judge on *Shark Tank*, and he may have been the first person ever to grace the cover of *Forbes* wearing a cowboy shirt. A former Google executive, Sacca left the company to "reinvent the way venture capital is done."[41]

Chris has an unsurpassed record of getting in early—and getting heavily involved—on some of today's most successful start-ups. His portfolio includes Blue Bottle Coffee, Instagram, Kickstarter, Stripe, Twilio, Twitter, and Uber. What entrepreneur would not want to join this list? Sacca's enviable track record led *Forbes* to place him in the number-two position on its annual "Midas List" of investors—those for whom seemingly everything they touch turns to gold. They even put him on the cover—for a VC, that's bigger than being on the front of *Rolling Stone* or *People*.

What drives Chris as he considers what he will invest in next? One of the biggest factors is purpose.

How Did Our Family Make All This Money?

Chris explained his approach to investing to me in a long and enlightening phone interview from his ski home in Lake Tahoe:

My wife Crystal and I make all investing decisions together. Sure, we evaluate the product and the team building it and use our experience to suss out if it will make money. But each time we also ask ourselves, 'Will we be proud to say we are investors in this company?'

We have three daughters who are now 6, 4 and 2, and one day when they inevitably ask, "Mom and Dad, how did our family make all this money?" we want to be proud of our answer.

So, Kickstarter, as one example, was a natural, as it's allowing thousands of creative and artistic people to get funding to pursue their dreams. And by the way, it's already paying sizable dividends to us despite being a B Corp.

At the same time, Chris and Crystal turned down investments where "we thought the returns would be no-brainers, but the business model would not make us proud. For instance, there was a site where teenagers could ask their network of friends to rate how hot they looked," he said with a laugh. "They had a ton of users and were growing like a weed, but we thought, 'Shouldn't we be encouraging kids everywhere to think that the more important ratings were the ones they'd find on their report cards?'"

Chris can talk a mile a minute, which is a good thing because I've long believed that more he talks, the smarter I get. I asked him about some of the more little-known investments he had made, and whether purpose had driven any of those decisions.

You know what's a great company? StyleSeat. It might sound funny, but it's essentially Uber for stylists. We went into that deal because we knew and admired the founder, Melody McCloskey, but the company had so much more depth than we realized. Beauty professionals are mostly women, and about half of them are women of color, and StyleSeat has turned out to be this incredibly liberating platform that allows these women to own their own businesses.

The economics for stylists used to be such that you'd pay significant rent for a chair at a salon; it's a bit like the taxi system, where a taxi driver pays upfront for the use of the cab medallion that night. The driver might make that night, but in the end, they have no real ownership or equity in the business. It's the individual who owns the medallion who makes the rules and reaps much of the economic rewards. The drivers have no real customer base.

Similarly, the salon stylists have to rent the chair and give the salon a percentage of what they make. Honestly, it reminds me a bit of indentured servitude. StyleSeat has allowed these women to instead own their own business. A lot of the women doing braids and weaves in the African-American community do it right from their home, and they own their business now.

Almost all of Melody's management team are women, and specifically women who came to work there from incredibly cool gigs at some of the biggest companies in the world. They do this because they know they're going to have a meaningful and positive impact.

They've realized, just as Crystal and I have, how much StyleSeat empowers the women who use it and how it changes their lives. We continue to grow prouder of what this company is doing to create business opportunities for women. I think the investment will do well for us, but just as important to us is knowing that these entrepreneurs are now making much better money and have much more control over their own destiny.

Sacca is a unique guy, but his interest in purpose-driven investments is not. In fact, we increasingly see purpose being used as a "marriage broker." When the best companies have choices, and the best investors do too, each side's commitment to purpose can be a powerful magnet that brings them together. I know of no better story to illustrate this than the one involving an old friend of mine selling his start-up to Howard Schultz, the founder and purpose-driven CEO of Starbucks.

Water, Water Everywhere: The Founding of Ethos

You may not have never heard of Peter Thum and Jonathan Greenblatt, but the chances are strong that you've seen their creation at Starbucks. Thum was a consultant at McKinsey who one day tripped across an opportunity that would become an inflection point he'd never imagined.

His catalyst occurred while working on a consulting project in South Africa in 2001. He noticed that hundreds of people didn't have access to the safe drinking water that he took for granted and could easily grab from the hotel's filtered water system or from the handy minibar. As he talked to people and began reading about this issue, he became motivated to act:

"The water problem was vast but subtle. It's not that unusual to hear of a two-year-old child dying of diarrhea. More than one billion people worldwide have no access to safe water. More than two million people die each year from illnesses related to unsafe water. Children die in disproportionate numbers because their immune systems are not fully developed."[42]

As luck would have it, his next consulting project involved advising a soft-drink manufacturer in the UK. He learned that bottled water was a fast-growing, $35-billion-a-year global industry. He also noticed that "people in England were willing to pay more for premium-branded water. I wondered whether there was a way to leverage this luxury industry to address a problem for people at the other end of the economic spectrum. If people were willing to pay a premium for water named after its source, wouldn't they want to pay for a brand devoted to funding humanitarian water programs?"[43]

The idea for Ethos was born. Thum would create the first bottled-water company that built a charitable donation stream into its business plan. Fifty percent of all profits would be donated to clean-water projects in locations ranging from Honduras to Kenya to of course South Africa, with the other 50 percent being returned to the company shareholders. This was a radical notion in 2002—that a company could be "for profit" but not focused *only* on profitability. Thum hoped to attract investors by convincing them that they could still make a decent return while also doing substantial good for the world. All those kids dying of easily preventable issues like diarrhea? The company would change all that!

Like most entrepreneurs, Thum knew that getting a company off the ground was a heavy lift and could be a lonely experience. He reached out to his roommate from his days at Northwestern's Kellogg Graduate School of Business, Jonathan Greenblatt. "He literally pitched me at my own wedding," Greenblatt remembers with a chuckle. Jonathan is a man of extremely high energy and intense focus—like a hypercaffeinated meerkat. He pounds the table when he makes a point that he particularly relishes. When he heard his old roommate's pitch, he was immediately sold. They both quit their jobs, jumped out of the airplane, and prayed that the parachute would deploy. Their new (and potentially less lucrative) lives would be all about "ethics in a bottle."

They hoped to differentiate their brand via their dedication to the mission of clean water and use this to achieve several business objectives:

- **Shelf space**: Water was a crowded market full of big players. If they were just another for-profit brand, it was likely very few retailers would give them a hearing. Helping kids in Africa and Central America might be the best pitch to get their foot in the door.

- **Consumer loyalty:** Who did a consumer help if they drank Evian or Perrier? A giant corporation. But every time they enjoyed Ethos, they could picture helping people in poor communities to have that same access to clean water. And that would feel good enough to be habit-forming.

Jonathan later recalled for me that it was the mission that gave them the courage to get started. "To us, it didn't matter if we built the biggest water company in the world. If our goal had been to beat the major players, we'd have been so intimidated, we would have never gotten started. So instead we made it our goal to just sell enough water that we'd help a few hundred communities."

They began the search for capital by making a list of everyone they knew who could connect them to potential angel investors or venture capitalists. Over the first months, they talked to over 150 potential investors. They were turned down by every one of them. The two budding water entrepreneurs were told that their payout ratio to the cause was too high and that the water market was very crowded; they'd be competing against goliaths like Nestlé, Coca-Cola, Pepsi, and Danone. Thum also speculates that "the fact that we were first-time entrepreneurs didn't help either."

Not all the rejections were friendly ones. Thum recalls visiting the mansion of a well-known venture capitalist. "A staffer offered us a seat on a couch that was probably worth more than Ethos's balance sheet. A half hour into the interview, the investor interrupted and advised us to start a 'real' company."[44] Greenblatt later recalled to me that another potential investor had told him, "'You know, you should consider joining the Peace Corps.' These perspectives echoed the views of most VCs at the time: philanthropy is philanthropy; business is a business."[45] Greenblatt recalls that "It was annoying that some of the investors didn't get it, but thankfully the consumers did. So, if I drink this water, other people get clean water. We were very early in linking consumption to cause."

The partners decided to self-finance the business. Like many "bootstrap" operations, their immediate focus was on keeping their costs as low as possible. With low sales volumes projected for the early years, they decided to save the capital expenditure necessary for certain machinery—with the result that the cofounders were personally screwing on the lids to each bottle! Their delivery vehicle was an old Volvo station wagon borrowed from a friend of Thum's mother.

Initial sales were slow, but each sale felt like a validation, an encouragement that someone else believed in their model enough to choose their product over a better-known (and much better-capitalized) brand like Evian or Perrier. And despite continually dipping into their own savings and losing money on each bottle sold, they stayed true to their mission and gave away the "profits" before there were any, choosing to fund a water-filtration system in a rural village in Honduras.

Every successful entrepreneur will fondly remember, and loves to recall, the biggest inflection points—those unexpected and often serendipitous events that can forever change the company's future. For the Ethos cofounders, it involved the Oscars. In 2003, the Oscars had a green theme, and the celebrity chariot was no longer a gas-guzzling limousine but instead a Prius. The organizers had heard about Ethos and offered to stock the water, waiving the traditional product-placement fee. Jonathan told me, "Nobody would do that for Coca-Cola—why would you do that when that means you're just making rich people richer? But they did it for us because they liked that we were so purpose driven."

That purpose-driven Oscars exposure led to celebrities like Kate Hudson appearing in magazines carrying Ethos and even a call from

Pierce Brosnan asking how he could get the water onto his yacht. The cofounders parlayed this exposure into pitch meetings with natural-food stores in the LA area, and the early take-up eventually landed them with their dream account: Whole Foods.

Then came the next big break—an invitation to take part in the prestigious annual TED conference. The dynamic duo arranged for a bottle of Ethos to be in every gift bag. They proudly donned their Ethos T-shirts and built a display showing the young children who were already benefitting from their first project. In an interview, Jonathan recalled for me their attempt to find prominent investors: "You're not supposed to pitch at TED, but we pitched like Nolan Ryan. I remember chasing Steve Case the wrong way up an escalator."

He was excited when eBay founder and original CEO Pierre Omidyar and his wife, Pam, stopped by the booth:

I struck up a conversation about Tufts—knowing that we all happened to be alumni—and soon we were talking about the bottles and brochures assembled on the table. Peter and I shared our story, explaining the core concept of the business and attempting to communicate our need for funding without explicitly saying so.

Pam and Pierre seemed interested, but so did many people at TED, which can feel like a carnival of entrepreneurs and innovators. It was a robust conversation, but they eventually wandered off. So it was a pleasant surprise when, a few days later, we received a call from Mike Mohr, their financial adviser. He explained that they wanted to learn more, and that conversation kicked off a due-diligence process that concluded when Pam and Pierre invested in Ethos via their innovative financial vehicle, the Omidyar Network.

ON was a single organization that deployed capital in a highly unusual manner. Like a foundation, it made grants to nonprofit organizations that were making a difference, such as Kiva. But like a venture fund, it also made investments in early-stage companies creating change, such as Meetup. This two-checkbook model made

ON very different than peer organizations—but it fit perfectly for Ethos. They made a venture-style investment in our company. And their trust changed our trajectory, eventually leading to an introduction to Starbucks.

Pierre knew Howard because the Starbucks CEO had served on the board of eBay. We knew Starbucks because they clearly were the perfect channel to distribute Ethos. Peter had crunched the numbers and put together an amazing plan about how we could provide them with healthy margins even as we sold them the product at a reasonable wholesale price. Once we had negotiated a reasonable deal, we were surprised when they came back and asked whether we might be interested in an acquisition.

The typical exit for a ready-to-drink beverage company is usually an acquisition rather than a public offering. Big companies like Coca-Cola and Pepsi specialize in gobbling up small businesses with novel products, as it's a way of outsourcing their R&D. But we did not anticipate that it would happen quite so soon for our company. It was not an easy decision, but ultimately we reverted back to our core values and asked ourselves—would a purchase by Starbucks serve the cause of helping children get clean water? Ultimately we knew the answer was yes, and everything then fell into place.

Distribution would no longer be a problem for the company. Ramping up production to get product into over seven thousand Starbucks locations would be the new challenge. And that was just the start. Through a Starbucks distribution partnership with Pepsi, their little-known water that gave back would soon be carried in over one hundred thousand retail outlets, including Cost Plus and Target.

The Ethos cofounders had used their mission to win the ears of some of the world's most influential investors, and with that came a wider distribution for the product than they had ever thought possible. And the funding for clean-water projects would increase, as Starbucks increased the donation amount per bottle sold from just under two cents to five cents. Within a few years, the total investment in partners like Mercy Corps and UNICEF, who were implementing the clean-water projects, would exceed $10 million. As the business has grown, the payouts have increased—over $3.4 million was donated in 2014 alone.[46] If that can be sustained over the next decade, it will be one of the single largest sources of funding for water projects in coffee-growing countries.

Don't Show Me the Money. Show Me the Purpose!

The clear majority of millennial (88 percent) and high-net-worth (82 percent) investors surveyed by the global asset-management firm Legg Mason said environmental, social, and governance (ESG) investing was appealing. They realize that it's not a trade-off between money and meaning—it's a collaboration. And yet, less than 20 percent of high-net-worth and just over 10 percent of millennial investors said they had heard about ESG investments from their advisers.

I hear similar stories to those above more and more often, especially from seasoned veterans. "I'm looking for my next investments, but I want them to be something that does good for the world." As one of the leading private-equity start-up investors in Hong Kong told me:

> I'm old enough now and have made enough money that I don't have to do this anymore. When I was younger, I made money simply for the sake of making money and did not care that much about anything besides the ultimate ROI on the deal. I was kind of transactional and selfish.
>
> But now I've made a conscious choice—I will only invest in businesses where they can show me that there is a social purpose to the business. It's the first question I ask, and if they can't answer it, I immediately lose interest. But if they've got that part nailed, I will consider an investment, even if it means I accept a lower financial return.

Which raises the question...

Is a Lower ROI Inevitable?

When people talk about values-based investing, they sometimes create a false dichotomy. They assume that a socially responsible investment may have a lower yield than a more traditional investment that ignores social and environmental factors.

But rather than seeing a suboptimal return, in many cases, they see a higher one from their investments in purpose-driven companies. I asked Chris Sacca about this, and he proudly told me about an investment that was not only one of his favorite companies but also was providing outsize returns.

Our most profitable investment, on a per-employee basis [and based on] who's generating the most profitable cash returns, is actually Kickstarter. And yet Kickstarter is a public-benefit corporation—the type where your shareholders can actually sue you if you're not operating in the public interest.

We always knew they were a special company when we invested and that the founders thought differently about things. They said from the beginning that they were never going to sell the company and were never going to go public. That's usually a pretty hard sell for investors—because you're left wondering, so how am I going to get my money back?

But they successfully convinced a lot of top-shelf VCs—like Fred Wilson in New York—to invest in this company. Kickstarter just knew from the beginning that they wanted to be special and to value the community here and to manage the integrity of this platform rather than only pushing for quarterly earnings. They decided that's what it takes to make Kickstarter a place we're all deeply proud of.

So despite Kickstarter being both a public-benefit corporation and a tech company, we recently got a dividend from them, which has never happened in the history of any of my portfolio companies. They literally paid us, and we could opt in and get it in stock or cash. But they literally distributed a bunch of cash because Kickstarter is making so much money. And I think that's fascinating. From an investment perspective, obviously Uber will be our highest return percentage, but literally the healthiest and most profitable of our operating businesses is Kickstarter.

One Final Question...

Investors want to know how they can cash in on the fruits of your labor. You need only look at the recent phenomenon of big companies hungrily gobbling up smaller, socially responsible brands to know that purpose can up the ante. Take a look at this brief list of small organic companies that have been bought out by corporate giants:

- In addition to WhiteWave Foods, Danone also acquired Stonyfield Farm.
- General Mills bought Annie's Homegrown, a Berkeley, California–based maker of "natural" and organic pastas, meals, and snacks.
- Hershey's bought Dagoba Chocolate ("sourced with care") for $17 million in 2006.
- Kellogg's bought Kashi—a maker of a variety of organic, plant-powered products—for $33 million in 2000.
- The Coca-Cola Company purchased a 40 percent stake of Honest Tea at $43 million in 2008. It bought the rest of the company in 2011.

And this phenomenon isn't limited to edibles. Colgate-Palmolive acquired the environmentally focused Tom's of Maine for $100 million in 2006, and Clorox bought the beloved natural-product line Burt's Bees for $913 million in 2007.

One of the big questions facing these companies is whether they'll stay true to the original vision once they're part of a much larger company. The acquisition prices often have lofty assumptions about both revenue and profit growth built in to cash-flow scenarios, and there are usually no guarantees that the new owners won't play by new rules.

One way to mitigate this risk is to make sure your new owners are the *right* owners.

A Recipe for Success

A former punk rock musician and artist turned entrepreneur, Neil Grimmer cofounded the children's food brand Plum Organics in 2007. The expressed goal for the business was to not just sell baby food, but "to shape children's palates for a lifetime of healthy eating." Neil explains that the leadership team always approached the business as parents, rather than as executives. "You've heard the phrase, 'Hey it's nothing personal, it's just business'? I think that's one of the single most damning phrases in the business world today because the implication is that you're supposed remove your humanity from the equation." Neil was determined to change that, and prove that the future of business had purpose and profit inextricably linked.

He proved that and more. By 2013, the company had north of $90 million in sales. Plum was one of the fastest-growing companies in America at the time, which meant that Neil was suddenly inundated with inbound inquiries from companies throughout the world, interested in a possible merger or acquisition. One such company was Campbell Soup. A breakfast with President and CEO Denise Morrison was proposed for the Waldorf Astoria, and Neil figured it was his fiduciary responsibility to attend. But from the moment he met Denise, he could tell this would a different kind of conversation. Neil said:

> It was one of those moments where you realize that behind these big companies, there are people—and in this case an amazing person. The first thing Denise said to me was, "My grandkids aren't Gerber babies, they're Plum babies." She told me how she'd been sent to Whole Foods and Babies"R"Us at all hours of the night to restock on Plum products for her daughter, and that she understood why we were doing what we were doing.

Most of the meetings I was taking at the time involved someone saying to me, "Hey, we love your growth. How about you move into our headquarters, let us take over the reins, and call it a day?" But Denise talked a lot about the mission of our company, our shared interest in innovation, and the potential to impact lives in a broader way. She said, "Your path is clear and we don't want to get in the way. Just keep doing what you're doing over there in Emeryville, California, and let us know how we can help."

Three months later, Campbell Soup acquired Plum Organics for $249 million. Neil knows that some people consider that "selling out," but he protests that term and instead prefers "selling in."

We're at an inflection point where the big industry players, the ones that have some of the biggest impact in the world, are *truly* interested in adopting the values, and the mindset, the ethos, of these small more purpose-driven brands. It's not just about buying a sustainable company as a growth driver, but in an effort to shift the entire larger organization to a different way of thinking.

It's no accident that we were on Denise's radar. She'd already established the mandate that she wanted to transform Campbell Soup into one of the leading health and wellness food companies in the country. We became a part of that overall mission and a demonstration of how that is possible.

And Campbell Soup was true to its word. In fact, just a few days after the deal was closed, Neil had a meeting with Mark Alexander, who was the President of Campbell North America at the time. "On my punch list of things to discuss," says Neil, "was becoming a Public Benefit Corporation. I explained why it was critically important to Plum. This was all new terminology to Mark, but he did a lot of listening and head nodding, and at the end he said, 'Look, if this is something you would have done if you weren't owned by us, and it feels integral to your mission, I'll give it serious consideration." A few days later, Denise called and said, "We've got a bunch of questions, but we love this idea so let's try to figure it out." Within three weeks, we had new bylaws written for the company and we were the first founding public benefit corporation in the state of Delaware. It was incredibly exciting.

Recently Grimmer founded a new company called Habit, which combines nutrition, technology, and food delivery into one bundle. Its sole investor? The Campbell Soup Company, which invested $32 million this year.

Another risk mitigator is consumer vigilance. If these once-smaller and independent companies become part of the problem rather than part of the solution, it's likely that citizen regulators and social-media critics will waste little time making their opinions known. And in a world with more start-up companies than ever before, there's always the power of competition to allow purpose-driven consumers to have multiple options as they choose the companies whose values and mission most closely mirror their own.

Impact Investing

Perhaps the greatest proof that purpose and investment are no longer mutually exclusive—if they ever were—is the emergence of "impact investing."

According to the Global Impact Investing Network, impact investments refer to "investments made into companies, organizations, and funds with the intention to generate social and environmental impact alongside a financial return."[47] Apparently the term was coined in 2007, when the Rockefeller Foundation organized a gathering of leaders at Bellagio, its spectacular retreat high in the Italian Alps, to discuss a new form of financial investment that could achieve a social or environmental impact.

"There were green investors, there were microfinance investors, and, in the US, there were community-financed investors—we named all of this 'impact investing,'" says Bugg-Levine, who, as managing director of the Rockefeller Foundation from 2007 to 2011, designed and led its impact-investing initiative. "But more than the language, in 2007 we asserted that these different organizations and groups were part of a mind-set shift."[48]

Impact investment has attracted a wide variety of investors, both individual and institutional. Think-fund managers, development-finance institutions, diversified financial institutions and banks, private foundations, pension funds and insurance companies, family offices, individual investors, and religious institutions.

The Global Impact Investing Network conducted a survey this year in which respondents reported investing $22.1 billion into nearly eight thousand investments focused on positive impact and said they planned to increase that amount by 17 percent next year. Of course, this figure is small when held up against the trillions of dollars at play in global capital markets, but sustainable investing is going mainstream—just look at the new impact-investing units set up by BlackRock and Goldman Sachs.

Jean Case, CEO of the Case Foundation, which she began with her husband, Steve Case, cites the positive example of Revolution Foods, in which her husband is an investor. In the "B the Change" article, Case says that "they have returns that would turn the head of any early-stage investor." She believes they're demonstrating that it's a very real company while balancing the financial interest of its investors with the social impact it wants to have. Some even argue that a day will come when these kinds of investments will no longer need to be called "impact," because all businesses will consider the effect they have on people and the planet.[49]

But you might be wondering—is socially responsible investing a fad or part of the future?

The Next Generation: Values-Driven Investors

The amount of funding available for investment in mission-driven companies is already large, and every month it is increased dramatically. Why? Because over the coming decades, the biggest intergenerational wealth transfer in human history will occur. The amount of assets that will be handed from parent to child is estimated in the range of $30 to $59 trillion (trillion, with a *t!*).

This should be good news for mission-led companies, who will have access to an increasingly large pool of capital. Of all the generations alive today, millennials are the most willing to accept a lower financial return if it means a greater social impact. This is backed up by US Trust, a private bank serving the ultrarich. Their 2017 survey of nearly seven hundred high-net-worth adults found that seven in ten millennials view their investment decisions as a way to express their social, political, and environmental values. Seven in ten also believe that it is possible to achieve market-rate returns investing in companies based on their social or environmental impact.[50]

Rejecting Where the Family Money Came From

Justin Rockefeller recently sat down with the *Financial Times* and had this to say: "I want to build on the family legacy, and the best way I know how to do that sits at the intersection of philanthropy and capitalism. Impact investing continues both family traditions, but with a new spin on it. There is something in it for the G1, the grandparents," says Rockefeller. "The common gripe among them is, 'I can't get my grandkids to sit down and learn how to read a balance sheet.' And the reverse gripe among millennials is, 'I want to invest in companies that I think are making the world a better place, and I can't get my grandparents to abandon this traditional view of investing.' Impact investing has provided a bridge for intergenerational dialogue."

The Rockefeller Family Fund can dedicate a larger portion of its investment portfolio to impact investing these days because it has finally been able to divest itself of fossil fuels.

In March 2016, the Rockefeller Family Fund stunned the investing world when it announced that it would withdraw all investments from fossil-fuel companies, including ExxonMobil.

The Rockefeller family fortune, after all, was made by John D. Rockefeller and his descendants primarily through Standard Oil, a company eventually absorbed into Exxon. It was a move akin to the children of Bill and Melinda Gates divesting themselves of any shares in Microsoft. Citing the long-held allegations that the company had worked to suppress and obfuscate climate-change research, the foundation called ExxonMobil "morally reprehensible" and added, "There is no sane rationale for companies to continue to explore for new sources of hydrocarbons. We must keep most of the already discovered reserves in the ground if there is any hope for human and natural ecosystems to survive and thrive in the decades ahead."

The Rockefeller Family Fund acknowledged that the family had made a lot of money from oil, "but history moves on, as it must."

Exxon is a huge conglomerate and could console itself that someone else would buy the shares now made available on the open market. But in a world where trust and reputation greatly affect everything from consumer behavior to talent recruitment to employee morale, can they afford to ignore the psychological effect of such a high-level rejection?

Who Will Run the World? Girls!

When talking about the investors of the future, let's not forget the enormous gains that women have made in the space.

When impact investing first caught on, women and girls were arguably seen more as beneficiaries than decision makers. But today's reality is that women control slightly more than half of the private wealth in the United States and make 80 percent of all purchases. According to Boston College's Center on Wealth and Philanthropy, women stand to inherit 70 percent of the $58.1 trillion in intergenerational wealth transfer expected over the next four decades. Advances in education and higher labor-force participation, combined with generational and spousal wealth transfer, are leading some experts to predict that roughly two-thirds of the nation's wealth will be in the hands of women by 2030.

This avalanche of money will land in the laps of female investors, who have demonstrated a greater interest in social investing than their male peers. Half of wealthy women in a recent survey expressed an interest in social and environmental investing, while only one-third of wealthy men did. More than six in ten women thought social, political, and environmental impacts were important, as compared to just 52 percent of men.[51]

Two's Company, Three's Crowdfunding

Of course, any talk of the future of investing must also make mention of crowdfunding.

When we think of investors, we picture a well-heeled elite, sitting in glassy high-rises, tossing money to hungry start-up founders below. But as it has done with so much else in this modern era, the Internet is democratizing fund-raising too.

Granted, pledging money on Kickstarter does not make a person an "investor" in the traditional sense of the word; crowdfunding campaigns don't offer equity or any sort of return beyond the product featured. But it's built around the idea of advancing money, of committing early capital and helping to bootstrap a business that you believe in. As such, there are a ton of businesses that consider these platforms exactly the right avenue for securing those "sufficient funds in the start-up phase" that I mentioned in this chapter's introduction.

And what is this new breed of "next-door" investors looking for in potential investments? You need only refer to the chapter on

"Wooing the Customer" for some clues, because, ultimately, services like Kickstarter and Indiegogo are just simpler ways to buy and sell stuff.

Take LeVar Burton's *Reading Rainbow* Kickstarter, launched in May 2014. To date, more than one hundred thousand backers have pledged over $6 million to help bring this project to life, breaking the record for the most individual backers. When asked, "Who is the typical backer?" Burton said in a *Rolling Stone* interview, "The typical backer is in their early twenties to thirties, and they grew up on the show. They have a set of values that definitely includes altruism and personal responsibility for the world in which they live."

Drinking with Your Investors

Brian Smith might just have the best job in the world. When the cofounder and CEO of British Columbia–based Persephone Brewing Company meets up with his investors, he typically does it over a beer.

Persephone is the first and only Certified B Corp brewery in British Columbia. The eleven-acre farm and craft microbrewery is operated by a small team of extremely passionate people committed to the vision of "supporting amazing beer built through local agriculture, community connectedness, and partnerships." It uses a "farmhouse" approach to produce its award-winning craft beer, with on-site farming of hops and other food crops in support of local food security (i.e., "farm to table AND farm to barrel").

Persephone's offerings were very popular, perhaps as karmic payback for its choosing a name to honor the goddess of spring bounty. As a result, the company needed growth capital, and in 2014 it decided to take advantage of changes in securities laws that were for the first time allowing small investors to buy equity stakes in companies.

Equity investing isn't new, but in the past, it had been limited to "accredited investors," or wealthy people with a net worth of over $1 million. In theory, this was to protect the nonwealthy from bad decisions and financial ruin, but the flip side was that ordinary citizens were denied the opportunity to invest as they saw fit.

The UK was one of the first markets to find success with crowd-funding, as smaller producers realized their investors could become their customers and vice versa. If the business prospered, the average pub dweller would share in those rewards. Persephone took a similar approach. "I have a long history in the co-op movement," says Smith, "dating back to an earlier career in community economic development, and the co-op business model is particularly apropos if we are trying to achieve economic justice in our society." The team decided to capitalize the brewery as a for-profit social venture at first and democratize governance and ownership over time. "We wanted to make sure we were walking our talk and to articulate our value proposition internally and externally."

Research has shown that the newest generation of investors is the most eager in history to embrace investing in a way that maximizes social impact while also providing an acceptable ROI. Smith and his team are a prime example. Smith explained his experience: "There is absolutely no doubt that many of our investors have invested because we are a social venture. In fact, many don't even drink beer and participate solely because of our social, environmental, and community mandate. They are motivated by our social mission as well as the perceived promise of ROI, given the growth of the craft-beer sector."

The decision to embark on a crowd-funded model has put Smith in touch with an army of investors he might not have had access to otherwise. Look at his list of the key investor segments that comprise the brewery's ownership group:

Founders who identify as social entrepreneurs; friends and family who support social entrepreneurs; impact investors who support local ag and mission-based businesses; locals who support localization of our food system and economy; customers that love our product; customers that want to be a part of social change; and employees that are dedicated to the vision.

In short the people who own our company are invested and "invested" in the social mission. Many, maybe all of them, have visited our farm, and that first-hand experience is compelling, especially when it includes high-quality beer. If an investment includes a great story, social mission, excellent product, and market competitiveness, then people will (a) want to be a part of it and (b) invest.

What Kind of Conversations Do You Want to Have?

Having investors who are driven by purpose will also give you something to talk about in addition to just the usual financial numbers. Yes, those are important and can't be ignored. But when you and your investors are united not just around profits and cash flow but also around mission, it's a more enjoyable conversation—one that creates a different bond.

If your investors care about not just a fair return but also a social outcome, this can lead to a much more symbiotic and mutually supportive relationship. After all, growing and running a business is usually full of huge challenges. But when you're united with the right investors who share your values and cheer you on as you achieve both *social* and *financial* impact, that will make that long and shared road trip quite a bit more enjoyable.

And don't forget the alternative: if you have investors who are maniacally focused on one thing and one thing only—their own ROI— then you may find yourself in a world where "too much is never enough." That's the nature of greed, right? You might deliver to them a 15 percent return on their investment, and rather than be thanked, they will ask you, "How can you goose this to 20 percent?"

Investors—from individuals to institutional giants—are seeing the social and financial value of aligning purpose with profit, and it's increasingly important for your brand to define, measure, and share your purpose-driven mission, for the benefit of humanity and your bottom line.

Remember that investors are people too. And yes, you do have to "show them the money," and I don't suggest you perform the entrepreneurial equivalent of putting a flower in the barrel of their gun, but every one of us has a dinner-table conversation waiting for us at the end of our workday, where we process aloud to those we love what we've done and not done with our time. And none of us is just an employee—we're friends and parents and children and neighbors. And a bank account and the size of our house is no longer the only way we measure our success. The metrics have changed.

8

Risk Reduction and Avoidance of Regulators

Wait, wait! I know that's a boring chapter topic, but please stick with me. I want to make one last case for incorporating purpose into your business—and I promise it will be an interesting argument.

If you're a senior executive, the reasons to concern yourself with regulators is clear. If you hold a junior position or work at a smaller company that is not in the public spotlight, it might seem removed. But in this chapter, I'll explain why I think this is relevant for all. This includes the fact that it's not just governments that are now regulating businesses. I'll show examples of a new breed of "citizen regulator" (there are now millions of them watching the companies with which they do business) and also a growing movement of businesses regulating other businesses. The future will be even more transparent by the day, so regardless of your position or the size of your company, you need to know who's watching you!

You Can't Afford Not To

In our modern world, businesses have more watchdogs and regulators than ever before. Governments are ever vigilant, policing everything from automobile emissions to data protection to financial malfeasance. Those companies being run in an unethical manner face a daunting litany of repercussions, including whopping fines, restrictions on how they run their business, and increased cost (both financial and of bandwidth) to comply with increased regulation.

If you ask one hundred senior executives how many of them wish they could spend more time with government regulators, you likely won't see a single hand go into the air (and if you do, then you should possibly short their stock). The costs of government regulation include leadership bandwidth, legal fees, labyrinthine adjustments to systems of compliance, and sometimes heavy fines and penalties.

Wall Street banks are a classic case study in this area. Most of them failed by never building the case that they were about anything more than making rich bankers (and shareholders) richer. The fact that they never got out ahead of the curve on purpose was ultimately deleterious to their shareholders. For example, during just one year—2013—JPMorgan paid over $20 billion in fines for behavior that helped lead to the global financial crisis.[52]

The direct costs, while stratospheric, can be dwarfed by the intangible ones. When a company is under investigation by government regulators or has suffered heavy penalties, it can repel potential employees, demotivate current ones, alienate customers, and drive away prospects.

It also—let's face it—just really makes your job suck!

The Halo Effect of CSR

Companies that have earned the right to "wear haloes" are less likely to have leadership bandwidth chewed up by time-consuming regulatory regimes, to finance armies of high-priced white-shoe lawyers, and to lose both customer and employee confidence that often comes with accusations of unethical or illegal behavior.

This all sounds good, but is there data to back it up? Yes. In a 2015 paper titled "Crime, Punishment, and the Halo Effect of Corporate Social Responsibility," Princeton economists Harrison Hong and Inessa Liskovich studied how steeply US companies are fined by the Department of Justice and the SEC for bribing foreign governments. They found that the more socially responsible the company in question, the lower the fine they incurred. Improvements in social-responsibility activities were associated with $2 million less in fines. "We show that this bias is likely a halo effect and not a prosecutorial conflict of interest," they wrote. "One implication of our analysis is that firms might very well have a strategic motive to be socially responsible as a form of insurance in case of unfavorable regulation."

Social Issues Become Financial Issues

Being proactive on environmental issues can lower the costs of complying with present and future regulations, advises Novo Nordisk CEO Lars Sorensen. The Danish multinational pharmaceutical company's leader was rated the world's number one CEO in 2015 by the *Harvard Business Review*. His advice:

> If we don't treat employees well, if we don't behave as good corporate citizens in our local communities, and if we don't provide inexpensive products for poorer countries, governments will impose regulations on us that will end up being very costly. Corporate social responsibility is nothing more than maximizing the value of your company over a long period of time. In the long term, social and environmental issues become financial issues. There is really no hocus-pocus about this. If we keep

polluting, stricter regulations will be imposed, and energy consumption will become costlier.[53]

The Rise of B-2-B Regulation

Business executives should not expect scrutiny from only government regulators, though. As though that is not challenging enough, it's increasingly likely that they will also be judged and evaluated by other businesses. After all, if a whole new generation of companies are using purpose to recruit, motivate, and retain their best employees and to thrill their customers, they will have to show every day that they mean it. This means that they will not just be expecting "digital due diligence" from citizen regulators; they will also be performing their own due diligence on the companies with which they do business. As we saw with the way CVS turned its back on the tobacco industry, such decisions can have some outsize effects on other companies and whole industries. As another example, we'll review how a search engine closed the on-ramp for customer referrals to products that some viewed as being financially toxic.

Shutting Down the Payday Lenders

One of the most profitable niches of the finance industry has been short-term (also known as "payday") lenders. Payday loans are often the last-gasp attempt to gain short-term cash by people who live paycheck to paycheck, who have no savings, or who have maxed out their credit cards. The borrower often knows that the loans are not good for his or her own personal finances, but he or she uses them anyway when in a tight situation or jam. A borrower may pay a fee of $30 to borrow $200 for a week.

So, did that $200 car repair he could barely afford make any more sense now that it cost him $230? The lender would argue that it's a small price to pay for an essential service that allowed the lender to not miss a day of work or to avoid having the heat turned off during a harsh winter. Critics argue that a loan costing 125 percent, or four times the rate of even the most usurious credit card, is just another way the finance industry screws the poor.

The situation is even worse for those who can't afford to pay the loan back, as they can then be charged numerous late fees and "interest on interest" on a loan that refuses to go away. A 2014 study by the Pew Charitable Trusts estimated that the typical online payday lender charged an annual percentage rate of 650 percent and found that one in three customers said they caught an online payday lender making an unauthorized withdrawal from their account.[54]

Those lenders often found new customers online by buying keywords on search engines. They were caught off guard in May of 2016, when Google announced that it would no longer sell advertising to the industry.

Quick-fix loans charging triple-digit rates seem to be viewed by Google and others now with the same social stigma as other dangerous products banned from advertising, such as cigarettes.[55]

David Graff, the director of global product policy at Google, announced in a blog post that the global ban would apply to loans for which repayment was due in sixty days and for loans that carry an annual percentage rate of 36 percent or higher. His rationale was that the change was "designed to protect our users from deceptive or harmful financial products. Ads for financial services are an area of vigilance given how core they are to people's livelihood and well-being. Research has shown that these loans can result in unaffordable payment and high default rates for users."

Whether you agree with Google or not, it's important to note that something happened here that has historically been extremely rare: a business made the conscious decision to regulate other businesses—or more accurately, *to regulate an entire industry*. The decision was made by a small number of executives, but they control 93 percent of the online search market—as near a monopoly as found in any industry. Imagine if your country had ten airlines, and nine of them put you on their no-fly list—how much more difficult would that make it to run an efficient operation?

It was likely not an open-and-shut case. After all, the profitability on payday loans was so great that lenders were willing to pay Google up to twelve dollars *for every click-through* to their sites. Search-engine experts estimated that *loans* was the second most profitable search term for the company, behind only another granddaddy: *bankruptcy*. Did Google give up this easy money for purely ethical reasons?

Some speculated that Google's own idealistic employees might have put quiet pressure on the company. After all, if they had joined based partly on the embrace of working for a company with a deep social mission, how could they remain silent while watching their employer create instant connections to lenders viewed as being unscrupulous?

Saying No to Coal

Driven by pressure from employees, companies have begun to audit their entire supply chain. After all, it's illogical to say your company is mission driven if it's buying from suppliers who aren't. This includes the banking industry, which can influence other businesses and industries through the denial of financing.

Responding to pressure from both shareholders and consumers concerned about the effect the burning of coal has on global warming, and pressured by environmental groups like the Rainforest Action Network, some of the world's biggest banks have recently announced that they will no longer provide financing to electricity plants that are coal fired. The group includes a who's who of the big American banks: Bank of America, Citibank, Deutsche Bank, JPMorgan, Morgan Stanley, and Wells Fargo.

According to Bloomberg, the divestment campaign's goal to help the world move beyond fossil fuels delivered still another blow to an industry already struggling through its worst downturn in decades. Coal is under siege from cheap natural gas stealing market share at power plants, tougher emissions standards, and slowing global demand. The combined market capitalization of US coal miners since 2011 has plunged from $74.4 billion to less than $7 billion [in March 2016].

Chiza Vitta, a metals and mining analyst with the credit-rating firm Standard & Poor's, commented, "There are always going to be periods of boom and bust. But what is happening in coal is a downward shift that is permanent."[56] Shortly after JPMorgan signed on to the list, the world's largest private-sector coal company, Peabody Energy, said that it might have to file for bankruptcy protection. They would be following a path already taken by three of the nation's other large coal companies.[57]

The *New York Times* reported that not every reason to pull back from coal was an altruistic one:

Some banks say they are trying to do their part to curtail climate change by moving away from coal projects and financing ventures that produce less carbon. But bankers also say there is a more basic reason for the shift: Lending to coal companies is too risky and could ultimately prove unprofitable. Coal companies are being squeezed by competition from less expensive energy sources like natural gas and by stiffer regulations—pressures that show no signs of letting up.[58]

In October 2017, the French bank BNP Paribas went even further, pledging to no longer finance shale and oil sands projects or do business with companies whose main activity stems from oil and natural gas obtained from shale or oil sands. The bank cited its commitment to international efforts to reverse global warming and stated that this goal can only be achieved by reducing the world's dependence on fossil fuels, especially from sources that emit high levels of greenhouse gases and harm the environment in other ways. It went further to say that it is its responsibility as a bank financing economic development in the 21st century to act as an accelerator of the energy transition.

I asked BNP Paribas's Asia-Pacific region CEO and member of the Executive Committee, Eric Raynaud, about the implications of this decision. Wasn't it difficult, in a competitive banking industry, to willingly turn away so much potential business? He responded, "We told our team that we can't say in public that we're so committed to sustainability, and then continue to operate in ways that harm the planet. We have hired great people, and I tell them, 'Go find business for us in solar, go find opportunities in renewables.' And while these adjustments are never easy, they have done just that."

Friends of Sharks

Increasingly, the pressure for businesses to regulate other businesses might start with consumers. A recent example from my home city of Hong Kong occurred during 2016, when the hometown airline, Cathay Pacific, found itself under tremendous consumer pressure to stop doing business with companies shipping shark fin on cargo flights. Shark-fin soup is an ancient delicacy in China, but it has become controversial. As wealth has risen rapidly in China, more and more people were able to afford this previously unattainable delicacy, leading to serious overfishing and putting many species of sharks on the endangered list.

Critics made two arguments. First, the cruelty involved—fins are sliced off the shark, with the rest of the carcass thrown back into the ocean like trash (analogous to the initial settlers to the American West, who would shoot a six-thousand-pound buffalo, cut out the tongue, and leave the rest of the animal to rot). Second, they argued that the fin is tasteless anyway; it's made mostly of cartilage, and its only purpose in the soup is as both a thickening agent and a status symbol. Why be cruel to an animal and put entire species at risk, they asked, for something you can't even taste?

Protesters asked Cathay Pacific to follow the lead of its smaller rival, Hong Kong Express, in banning the shipment of shark fin. Cathay agreed to allow shipments of shark fin only if it came from sustainable sources, but activists argued that it was almost impossible to tell if each fin was or was not sourced in this manner.

No matter who was right, an airline that makes 75 percent of its revenues from passengers and only 25 percent from cargo could not afford the negative publicity that came from online petitions and demonstrators dressed in shark suits staging protests at Cathay check-in counters.[59] And as we know from the social-media chapter, these images and videos can spread quickly and go viral.

One of the many people who stopped to take pictures at the airport, Lorainne Limchesing, told the *South China Morning Post* that she had not previously been aware of the airline's policy: "Cathay Pacific is a business-making airline, but they should heed their social responsibilities as well. They should follow suit if they care enough."[60]

The airline wasted little time and acted quickly. A spokesperson announced on June 23, 2016: "On the issue of shark's fin, with immediate effect, we are happy to agree to ban the carriage." Other airlines that have enacted similar bans include British Airways, American Airlines, Qantas, Singapore Airlines, and Emirates.

Everyone Is a Publisher, and Everything is Published

One of the biggest effects of handheld technology having become both powerful and ubiquitous is that there are more watchdogs than ever before. Today, everyone is a publisher, and everything is published. Run a hotel? Hundreds of people are posting their opinions of it on Trip Advisor. Own a restaurant? The service and the food are being praised or trashed on Yelp. On a hiring spree? Any recruit can go on Glassdoor to learn how your current and former employees feel about working for you. And as we saw in chapter 3, on social-media buzz, they're also not afraid to praise you if you're doing good things for the world and to trash you if you're not.

In the old days, you could make an educated guess about what would remain private and what would go public. Today that's not an option. Just assume it will all be public—especially anything that stands as an outlier (for being either exceptionally good or horribly bad).

The Rise of the Citizen Regulator

Social psychologists predict that over the next decade, the world will see a new generation of "citizen regulators." Billions of these smartphone-equipped consumers will be downloading a new generation of apps that measure and report on a variety of issues ranging from food safety to air quality to automobile emissions—even their own personal carbon footprint.

The sensors and monitors being built into today's mobile-phone technology are much more complex than most people realize. And with Moore's law continuing its inextricable march, the power of the phone to monitor and measure what's going on around it will only continue to accelerate. And it's not just phones—think about how cameras are everywhere, and it's a virtual certainty that in the continued quest for "security," they will become even more ubiquitous.

And who will be buying and using all that technology? A new generation that has historically low levels of trust in pretty much every old-line institution—government, organized religion, even traditional models of education. For business leaders, the biggest challenge is that this mistrust also extends to them. The younger the American voter, the more likely he or she was to "feel the Bern" and support the self-proclaimed socialist Bernie Sanders. It's certain that if they have an easy way to police all the world's "evil capitalists," they'll gladly dive right in.

Fifty Billion Regulators?

How many devices might be out there tracking your company's every move? How about fifty billion? That is not a typo. The *Wall Street Journal* recently predicted that "by 2020, the number of thermostats, pressure gauges, accelerometers, acoustic microphones, cameras, meters, and other measuring devices linked to the Internet is predicted to reach 50 billion worldwide."[61]

Minerva Tantoco, New York City's chief technology officer, explains, "We are entering an era where everything can have an Internet IP address, [and] where everything can be a censor. This is creating a mesh of connectedness we have never had before."[62]

Right now, someone is working on an application that will be made available to owners of VWs and Audis. It will continually track emissions and report (to the driver, to social media, perhaps even to the environmental-protection authorities) if the emissions exceed the public standards.

Governments are encouraging this new breed of citizen regulator. Elizabeth Warren, the architect of the US Bureau of Consumer Financial Protection, announced an initiative in 2015 under which the US government would adopt the latest crowd-sourcing technology to collect tips from millions of consumers about deceptive new financial practices. They'd be encouraged to report on anything that looked or felt suspicious—ranging from misleading mortgages to usurious interest rates to improper "gotcha" fees on credit cards.

Digital Due Diligence

Anticipating this tsunami of citizen regulators, a *Harvard Business Review* article titled "Is VW's Fraud the End of Large-Scale Corporate Deception?" advised C-suite executives to "consider digital due diligence emerging as the new normal for the sharing economy. Your best customers increasingly have the ability and incentive to become your worst enemies, should you deceive them."

The author of that article, Michael Schrage, is a research fellow at the MIT Sloan School's Initiative on the Digital Economy. He's an angel investor and has served on the board of publicly traded companies. He tells me, "Digital platforms in general—and 'social media' in particular—enable and empower consumers to publicly look out for themselves and each other's best interests. People become guardians who can wield the knife, sword, machine gun or nuclear weapon of viral—and global—negative publicity and warning. Anyone with a good story and decent evidence has the power to tarnish—and possibly ruin—an enterprise reputation."

He continues, "Individuals' complaints can quickly be aggregated, collated, and synthesized into legal/regulatory action by the state. An *Unsafe at Any Speed*, Ralph Nader could only dream of such an informed and empowered consumer citizenry."

Trust and Brand Value

Back in the old days, a company's market value was almost completely tied to its tangible assets—machines, physical plants, buildings, inventory, cash, and investments. Intangible assets—like the value of the brand—hardly mattered. In 1975 tangible assets comprised 83 percent of the S&P 500 market value; *intangible* assets comprised a mere 17 percent. By 2015, though, tangible assets made up only 16 percent of the S&P 500, while intangible assets made up 84 percent. This complete reversal goes to show that people, human beings, are the greatest driver of corporate value.

What exactly forms all that intangible value? The *Harvard Business Review* reports:

> Some of it is intellectual property. For consumer-facing companies, though, a vast amount of value resides in the brand value, an amorphous measure of how a company's key stakeholders—its customers and

employees foremost—feel about the company or product. Among the many emotions and feelings that tie us to brands, trust is one of the most foundational.

Trust can take decades to build but can be lost in hours. Leaders will have to be constantly vigilant in a world of fifty billion devices in the hands of an empowered but suspicious generation.

One day while in transit, I read a BBC story about one of the most famous "citizen regulators" of the last decade. Once I heard his story, I knew I needed to interview him, and thankfully he was willing to tell me the story of how he brought one of the world's largest automobile manufacturers to its knees.

Just a Simple Engineer from Michigan

John German does not look like a giant slayer. Slight of frame, with gray hair and glasses, he calls himself "just a simple engineer from Michigan." German works as the US colead of the International Council on Clean Transportation (ICCT), a not-for-profit organization dedicated to reducing vehicle emissions. More importantly, he's the one who discovered VW's "defeat device" and reported it to the US Environmental Protection Agency (EPA) and the California Air Resources Board (CARB).

German did not set out to defeat Volkswagen—he told me in our first phone interview that he was instead hoping to learn from them. "We had this bright idea that no one's tested diesel in the US. We thought the diesel in the US would be cleaner [than those in Europe], in part because the US standards are more stringent and because EPA and CARB have a history of enforcing defeat devices. Our plan was to take the data [from the United States] to Europe and say, 'Hey, they can do this in the US; why can't we do it in Europe?'"

They did not have the equipment needed to do the testing ("It's a half-million piece of equipment") but found a cheaper solution. "We put out a contract bid. Three organizations responded, and we selected West Virginia University. We paid them $70,000 to do the testing and to write up the report." The team at WVU modified an emissions-testing machine, placed it in the car trunks of a VW Passat, a VW Jetta, and a BMW X5, and dropped a probe into the exhaust pipe.

What they found, German told the BBC, was explosive:

> The team at WVU thought there was something wrong with their equipment, so they kept recalibrating, but they kept getting the same results. We found high—very high—emissions in the real-world tests. The Passat had emissions five to 20 times the standard. The Jetta was worse. It was 15–35 times the standard."

At this stage my goal was to turn the data over to the EPA and CARB and let the experts evaluate it. We discussed how much publicity we should give to the report. At one point we considered not even posting it online. What we finally compromised on was to publicize the data online, but we did not identify the manufacturer—we simply called them vehicles A, B, and C. We put it on the website and sent the study to the EPA and CARB to say, 'We think you should look at this.' Proving that he did not have an ax to grind, he "sent a courtesy copy to VW two days before we posted it, saying, 'I think this might be of interest, and by the way, vehicles A and B are yours.'

A Sixteen-Month Wait

And then...he waited. And waited some more. He heard back from Volkswagen, "thanking me, and saying that they would let us know, but I never heard anything from them after that." I asked if their lack of reaction caught him off guard, and he replied, "No, it didn't surprise me because I was almost certain it was a defeat device, so VW was in trouble and had internal issues to go through." He shared his bombshell with nobody other than his wife. "She was the only one I ever told. I was worried that VW could squash us like a bug."

But there was more interesting news from the regulators: "Every three to four months, I'd send an email to CARB and EPA asking for a status report, but I'd hear nothing back. Now I had spent thirteen years working at the EPA and knew that was a good sign, because if they have an active investigation going, they're not allowed to talk to outside parties."

During this time, VW was only digging itself a deeper pit. German was later to learn the full details, and he told me:

> The agencies went through sixteen months of VW flat-out lying and trying to obstruct their investigation. And that's why they got hit so hard. To give you an example of what was going on, VW did not say, 'We see the emissions are high, and we'll do what's known as the field fix,' which is where they notify the customers, who bring the cars in, and they fix the issue. They issued notice of the field fix in December of 2014, and they assured the agencies that this was going to fix the problem. Five months later CARB went out and acquired some of the vehicles with the 'fix' and tested them. The emissions had come down only a little bit—still way above the legal limits—so they [the regulators] hauled VW back in.
>
> Of everything that VW did, the thing that's most incomprehensible to me is that the agencies gave them a chance to get out of this easily. If VW had gone out there, removed the defeat devices, and made some hardware changes, then no one would have ever known—this would not have happened. Sure, there would be some fines, some remedy fees, some very small-stakes stuff compared to what eventually happened. And yet they continued to lie and to cheat and to try to get away with it. From my point of view, it was incomprehensibly stupid.

After sixteen months of waiting, German one day received a heads-up email from the EPA, letting him know that the next day they'd be announcing their findings. The simple engineer from Michigan was besieged with media requests, with his silence replaced by what he describes as "my fifteen minutes of fame."

For Volkswagen, the only results were infamy, a stock price that dropped by 40 percent, and a seemingly never-ending series of fines and penalties. In October 2017, Reuters estimated the total bill for the scandal to be north of $30 billion.[64]

As much as government regulators can be ever vigilant and often a thorn in the side of companies, they may be nothing compared to what comes next.

Warren Buffett has famously advised that if a leader ever faces a moral quandary, there is a simple way to decide: "Ask yourself how you would feel if whatever action you take or decision you make would appear on the front page of the next day's *New York Times*."

Thirty years ago, people's reaction to his homespun advice might have been to agree with him but to also think (and possibly rationalize), "But that will never happen to me." People often perform unethical acts or run unethical companies with the expectation that they won't get caught.

Nobody expects to get caught. And yet—they do! And that's OK if you're not doing anything wrong. But our media seem to be filled with constant examples, ranging from now-disgraced FIFA chief Sepp Blatter ("Hey, where did all those bricks of cash in my freezer come from?") to serial sexual harassers like Fox News chief Roger Ailes and now-disgraced Hollywood producer Harvey Weinstein.

If your company lacks a social mission or allows its people to operate in ethical gray areas, then what comes next will scare you.

The VW Fiasco: Too Legit to Quit

John German set a powerful domino effect in motion, and it was one that many others carried the banner for. I spoke with Frank O'Donnell, the founder of Clean Air Watch, who gave me the whole scoop:

I first learned of the looming scandal Friday morning, September 17, 2015. I was tipped off by a government source who was privy to the news but not authorized to speak on the record. At that point, I was told that the US EPA and Justice Department were planning to issue a seemingly obscure item called a "notice of violation" to a major car company.

After doing a bit of questioning, I determined that this case involved diesel engines and that the likely company involved was Volkswagen (which, at that time, was engaged in a high-profile television ad campaign touting how "clean" diesel cars are and how it was an "old wives' tale" to say they are dirty.

When I heard the news of this "notice of violation"—which the government appeared to be downplaying by slipping out a jargony statement on a Friday (usually a graveyard for news)—I thought, "Holy crap—this is big news—one that completely undermines this ad campaign and the whole idea of "clean diesel."

I was also, quite frankly, angry to think that our government seemed ready to downplay the significance of this case. So, I took some action. I called several key reporters: Joby Warrick of the *Washington Post*, Coral Davenport of the *New York Times*, Matthew Day of Associated Press, and Gabe Nelson of *Automotive News*. I told them all that I believed a major scandal was looming involving Volkswagen and cheating on emission tests. I urged all of them to start calling the EPA and Justice Department and ask what the heck was going on. None of them had an inkling of this before my call. At this point, the government had not notified anyone that it was even planning a press event.

Within hours in response, the federal government did call an actual news conference to announce the action. The news conference helped prompt worldwide attention, obviously. One of my US EPA contacts was shocked that so much attention was suddenly being paid to this. They clearly did not anticipate it.

Typically, once something produces headlines like this in the *New York Times*, television and other media elsewhere follow, which they did.

Obviously this corporate deception went very high up in the chain of command. Top VW officials either knew of it or conveniently decided not to know. To this point, VW was growing fat and happy because European governments—quite mistakenly, in my opinion—were promoting diesel cars as a solution to climate change. European emission enforcement had been very lax, and so I think VW believed it could fool US regulators.

There are longer-term repercussions. The idea of diesel cars as an antidote to climate change is now seen as foolish—even in Europe, as some cities are now banning diesel cars. VW itself is now touting the idea of electric cars.

As for other companies, I would hope they'd learn a lesson: cheaters don't win in the long run. And the public might not be as stupid or gullible as you think. There are people out there who not only want good corporate behavior but good government to keep companies in line.

I am almost always a glass-half-full optimist and a believer in capitalism, so it's a bit unusual for me to write a chapter with so many negative stories. But these are important examples to share, as we all need to be aware that today's world is full of all kinds of regulators, and that is only going to continue to increase as electronic devices become more powerful, sensitive, and ubiquitous.

There may be people in your company who are the "one day-ers" vowing that *one day*—not quite sure when, but *one day*—they will embrace a deeper sense of purpose. These examples may speak loudly to those who are not yet converts to our cause, by showing what can happen to businesses and executives who are not seen as being good for society.

For those who are driven by purpose, there is no reason to worry. And unless you relish the idea of spending time in the negative miasma of constant regulation, it's one more reason to join the movement that unites cause and capitalism.

9

Mean It! The Dangers of Paying Lip Service

We treat others like we would like to be treated ourselves…We work with customers and prospects openly, honestly and sincerely. We are satisfied with nothing less than the very best in everything we do. We will continue to raise the bar for everyone.

— Excerpt from Enron's vision statement

On Friday, September 11, 2015, a PR team in Germany sent out a press release to media around the world that said, "The Volkswagen Group has again been listed as the most sustainable automaker in the world's leading sustainability ranking." The chairman, Martin Winterkorn, hailed it as a "great success for the entire team" and flagged the company's "full marks…in the areas of codes of conduct, compliance, and anticorruption as well as innovation management, climate strategy, and life-cycle assessment."

Exactly one week later, the Environmental Protection Agency announced that officials would be holding a press call and taking questions on "a recent development regarding a major automaker." John German just walked us through the rest of the story.

What made this turn of events particularly remarkable is that Volkswagen had been considered a "global leader in corporate social responsibility." Its 150-page annual report was full of affectionately described CSR initiatives. Press heralded the company as a "thought leader" and "change agent." In 2014 the company collected a "gold medal" for sustainable development from the not-for-profit World Environmental Center, and in 2015, the Reputation Institute, a New York reputation consultant, announced that VW had the eleventh best CSR reputation in the world.

And not to put too fine a point on it, but the story took a wonderfully ironic twist the weekend after the news broke. Commercials broadcast during NFL games that Sunday featured a new Audi ad boasting of "truth in engineering," and viewers of that Sunday night's Primetime Emmy Awards were treated to similarly mistimed Audi advertisements featuring Kermit the Frog singing "It's Not Easy Being Green" in regard to the carmaker's just-released hybrid vehicle.

The moral of the story? Purpose can act as a competitive advantage, but only if you *mean it*. Checking the CSR box is not enough. You must create a culture of strong vision and values and tell a consistent and cohesive story that is true to them.

Green Is the New Black

The term *greenwashing* was coined in the 1980s to describe when a company tries to portray itself as more environmentally concerned than it is. Almost four decades later, the practice has grown, with brands falling all over themselves to outdo one another with eco-credentials.

While some businesses are sincerely committed to making the world a better, greener place, there are too many others that see environmentalism as little more than a marketing gimmick.

"Social and environmental responsibility should not be a competitive sport," said Daniel Korschun, a professor of marketing at Drexel University who has studied greenwashing. "Not every company can have the smallest carbon footprint or donate the most to charity."[65]

In 2010, TerraChoice, a consulting firm that studied the phenomenon, found that over nine in ten "greener" products commit one or more of what they called the "seven sins of greenwashing." These sins ranged from offering no evidence and being too vague to out-and-out deceit.

With environmental trickery doing more damage than ever before, environmental group Greenpeace launched a "Stop Greenwash" website in 2008 "to confront deceptive greenwashing campaigns, engage companies in debate, and give consumers, activists, and lawmakers the information and tools they need to…hold corporations accountable for the impacts their core business decisions and investments are having on our planet."[66]

For a very long time, CSR has focused far more on theatrics than tangible results. Talk among "purpose" champions often centers on storytelling instead of substance.

The problem with that is that customers have a nose for this.

The Pepsi Problem

It was hard to miss the Pepsi Ad Fiasco of 2017, but in case you did, let me briefly recap. The commercial's official title was "Live for Now

Moments Anthem" (whatever that means); it featured reality star Kendall Jenner; and the intended takeaway seemed to be that we should all "join the conversation," forget our woes, and unite behind a can of soda.

In the two-and-a-half-minute television spot, Jenner ditches a modeling gig to join a protest. After sharing some very hip fist bumps with her fellow protestors (all of whom seem exceptionally well dressed and good-looking), the *Keeping Up with the Kardashians* star tries to defuse tensions with police officers by…handing one a Pepsi. Clearly, all the women's marches and police-brutality protests would be so much more enjoyable—and successful!—if only there had been soda.

It was meant to feel contemporary and plugged in, but audiences felt that it commercialized and trivialized social movements in the name of moving merchandise.

According to data from Amobee Brand Intelligence, after the ad went live, "digital content engagement around Pepsi increased by 366 percent in just a day, but 43 percent mentioned Black Lives Matter, 31 percent called the ad "tone-deaf" and 10 percent anointed it as the "worst ever." Amobee also looked at content engagement around the term "tone-deaf" during the course of the one day the ad was live, and found that 77 percent of digital content used the term mentioned Kendall Jenner and Pepsi.[67]

One of the most significant people to comment on social media was Bernice King, the youngest daughter of Martin Luther King Jr. "If only Daddy would have known about the power of Pepsi," she tweeted. It was liked over three hundred thousand times and enjoyed over one hundred sixty thousand retweets.

"A collective feeling of disrespect washed over many of the viewers from marginalized communities, creating a powder keg that resulted in a viral-advertising meltdown," explained senior partner and brand specialist Eric S. Thomas. "In a world where progressive millennials rule the Internet, it didn't take long for some of the more outspoken of us to catch wind, write think pieces, and attack the very core of the idea."

I asked Eric what advice he would give to companies looking to show consumers they mean it. He told me, "This generation of consumers has highly advanced BS radars and hate being sold to. Simply tell us why you matter, how you fit into our complicated lives, and let us make a decision."

He recommends "hiring for diversity, actual millennials, and telling stories that get to the core of our shared human experiences."

Indeed, 2016 saw quite a lot of brands fall from grace. Radley Yeldar's Fit for Purpose index is considered Europe's only extensive review of brand purpose and measures how well brands are putting purpose into practice. It puts out annual rankings of the top one hundred companies for purpose, and last year twenty-eight brands were kicked off the list. Many of these are high-profile players, with Johnson & Johnson, Apple, Orange, Volkswagen, Samsung, WPP, JPMorgan, and Carrefour among the outcasts. Doing purpose is much harder than most companies believe. It's one thing to pick an uplifting slogan, and quite another to entrench purpose at the heart of your organization.

And it's not just the customers that care whether you mean it. Employees do too.

It's What's on the Inside That Counts

A recent study looks at what happens when employees view an organization's corporate philanthropy efforts as either substantive or symbolic. (Substantive can be thought of as initiatives that are genuinely meant to support the common good; symbolic is self-serving and focused on enhancing reputation and profit.)

The researchers found that when employees attribute corporate social responsibility as substantive, benefits accrue to the individual and to the organization as a whole; however, when viewed as engaging in greenwashing, self-serving engagement in corporate social responsibility backfires: employee reactions are negative, and they may do less for the organization and label it as a "taker" rather than a "giver."

Imagine how employees across Volkswagen are feeling these days. Are they committed to the company? Do they say nice things about their place of work in social settings, like a barbecue or football match? Do you think they are coining the company a *taker* or a *giver*?

"We already knew that a company's corporate-social-responsibility engagement produces positive outcomes. Now, however, we see that a company jumping on the corporate-social-responsibility bandwagon just for show or greenwashing doesn't fool its employees," said Dr. Magda Donia, assistant professor at the University of Ottawa's Telfer School of Management and lead author of the *Applied Psychology: An International Review* study. She explained to me, "A company perceived as disingenuous undermines its own effort. When it comes to corporate social responsibility, the focus should be on the giving, not the getting. The best way to win is to truly give and let visibility and marketability follow."

Walking the Walk

To truly mean it, each of us will have to make tough decisions in our careers. Being committed to cause when it's easy is one thing. Do we dare to stay committed even when it requires difficult choices and potentially negative consequences?

One episode that happened in early 2017 convinced me that Elon Musk is one leader who most definitely is not faking it. Musk was an early addition to newly elected US president Donald Trump's business roundtable. A few corporate CEOs have caught flak from customers who do not like President Trump, with few examples of the negative backlash being more prominent than the "delete Uber" campaign called in response to Travis Kalanick's participation on the panel (the campaign also gained energy due to Uber's unwillingness to honor a strike called by New York City taxi drivers at New York's JFK Airport against Trump's Muslim travel ban).

Many members of the panel argue that they could get more accomplished "inside the tent" than they could by standing outside it with protest banners. Musk was once one of those leaders; he tried to convince the president to keep the United States committed to the Paris agreement (a pact to reduce global carbon emissions that the United States, along with roughly 190 other countries, adopted during the Obama administration).

After weeks of his theatrical attempts to keep them guessing on his position on the Paris climate accords, Trump announced that the United States would withdraw. Musk, a data-driven and evidence-seeking science geek if ever there was one, could not agree. In SolarCity and Tesla, he had built two companies that had based much of their raison d'être around combating global warming.

Trump's decision was announced on June 1.

Musk did not need to convene focus groups, call in outside PR agencies, or spend hours engaged in internal debates. On June 2, he tweeted: "Am departing presidential councils. Climate change is real. Leaving Paris is not good for America or the world."

What's Right for the Patient?

I periodically checked back in with Scott Ullem while writing this book, asking questions about his journey to a purposeful career. One thing I wanted to know was whether his actual experience had been close to the ideal he'd expected. He'd been told during interviews that the company always put the patient first—even above profits. They could talk the talk, but could they walk the walk?

Scott sat bolt upright in his chair, his eyes widened, and it looked like his heart rate had immediately increased. I wondered whether I'd hit a nerve. "I can give you a great example. Let me tell you about a revelatory experience I had earlier this year." Scott went on:

> Mike had called a meeting with me and three other execs to work through a really hairy set of issues related to litigation we were embroiled in. We were debating different scenarios and the pros and cons of each one. Each scenario had a direct influence on patients—specifically, what choices patients and physicians would have around what products were available.
>
> We were all going back and forth, back and forth. Nobody outside that room would have ever known what was discussed. But at one point in this heated conversation, Mike interrupted and said, "*All stop*. This is all well and good. You're talking about the bottom line and the potential media reactions. Put all that crap aside. Let's go back to one fundamental question: What's right for the patient? If that is the lens through which we view these decisions, how does that change things?"
>
> The whole room got immediately silent. Conversation just stopped. Mike's question just completely reset the conversation. My spine was tingling, just as it is now as I retell you the story.
>
> And so, when we say we put the patient first, I really believe this because Mike believes it. He said it at a time when he didn't need to say it—nobody outside the room would have ever known what we had discussed. It's not just something we say—this is the way we operate the company.

So, we've talked about the customers and the employees. Let's not forgot the third important leg of the economic tripod: investors.

When the Money Means It

Paying close attention to the actions of investors can provide an incentive to "mean it." Take the story of an investor who discovered that Lululemon was greenwashing, by claiming that one line of their clothes made with seaweed had health benefits such as releasing amino acids, minerals, and vitamins into the skin. The investor, poised to short-sell the stock, sent a tip to the *New York Times* that Lululemon's claims were false.

Lululemon's stock price fell 20 percent in the week following the release of the article in 2007.[68]

Have You Ever Faked It?

So, what can firms do to protect themselves from the same fate as VW or Pepsi? How can you tell whether you "mean it" *enough?*

I spoke with Zach Mercurio, speaker extraordinaire and the author of *The Invisible Leader: Transform Your Life, Work, and Organization with the Power of Authentic Purpose.* I had heard that he'd put together a handy list of ways to avoid what he calls "whywashing"—"the use of a purpose beyond profit solely to enhance the public image of a business." I found his mini-manual so helpful and sensible that I asked him if I could share it within the pages of this book. Without further ado, here are Zach's "Five Sins of 'Whywashing'":

1. The sin of purposeful branding without purposeful behavior is committed when a company adopts a purpose-beyond-profit branding strategy but does not align every aspect of its operations and behaviors with that purpose.

It's when a company like Wells Fargo touts (and trademarks) a "culture of caring" for others yet rewards self-serving sales goals as a measure of success.

Purposeful organizations determine their success by how their purpose is delivered, or proven, in the world. Can every person, at any level of your organization, know and feel why you exist after every physical or digital interaction? That is the standard of a purposeful enterprise.

2. The sin of recruiting for purpose but managing for results is committed when new employees, mostly millennials, are lured into an organization with the promise of a culture of purpose but once in the cubicle are evaluated solely by results. The rise of the beanbag chairs, ping pong tables, and slides in the office as recruitment and retention strategies are symptoms of this sin.

If your flashy and emotional digital marketing says you exist to "better people's lives," but you drive new hires into the ground with 80-hour workweeks, so they can "prove themselves," then you are not a purposeful business.

3. The sin of dropping purpose when times get tough is committed when market conditions aren't favorable and decisions that contradict purpose are made from fear.

An example of the opposite was when Southwest Airlines was pressured from investors and consultants to start charging for bags with allegations they were leaving upwards of $300 million per year on the table. CEO Gary Kelly, reflecting on the original purpose of the company, said that they would not charge for bags because it violated the reason the company was founded: "To democratize the skies."

He instructed his leadership team to find the money, so they didn't have to charge for bags. The team also believed in the purpose, so much so that even the toughest financial times didn't sway their decision. Not only did Southwest decide not to charge for bags, but they also created the very public and well-known "Bags Fly Free" campaign which ended up driving $1 billion of new revenue and taking even more market share.

Are your decisions rooted in purpose even when times are tough?

4. The sin of focusing on white-collar purpose is committed when companies focus only on connecting white-collar employees to its purpose.

About sixty percent of the US workforce are lower wage service workers often residing in Fortune 500 distribution centers and factories.

The search for meaning and purpose is fundamentally human. And every person, starting at the bottom of the organization, must be emotionally connected to why the organization exists on the planet. They must see their role as crucial to delivering the purpose beyond productivity and profit.

Do the people who touch your products or services *last* know and feel the organization's purpose? Do they know where the product goes? Do they know they make a compelling difference in human beings' lives?

Or do you think they "are just there for the paycheck?"

5. The sin of no proof is committed when the purpose of the company is not experienced through policies and procedures.

Patagonia offers an example of what proving purpose looks like. Being purposeful starts with putting your money where your purpose is. Part of Patagonia's purpose is to "cause no unnecessary harm…" And that purpose is proven in daily employee life, even in addressing the potential harm caused to working families from a lack of affordable childcare. Therefore Patagonia has provided onsite daycare and nursery services since the early 1980s.

And the results have been not surprising: 100% of the women who have had children at Patagonia over the past five years have returned to work, significantly higher than the 79% average in the US.

Purpose in organizations and life isn't always pretty or cheap. And if it is, you might be whywashing. Purpose takes hard work, strategy, and tough decisions. Often these decisions sacrifice material gain in the short term for an unwavering alignment with the reason you and your organization exist. An alignment that, in the long term, can produce powerful results.

Closing Thoughts

Sustainability, and the values that underpin it, must be properly integrated into a business. If unethical business practices are not addressed and rectified, the company is at risk of major financial consequences. VW serves as a timely reminder that it's fine to focus on rankings, reports, press releases, and awards. But fundamentally, it's the outcomes and impacts of sustainability that create and destroy shareholder value.

Volkswagen's drama sends a clear message to the sustainability crowd. Rather than competing for the best possible narrative, or focusing on the optics of 'doing good,' purpose-driven professionals must challenge each other and demonstrate they are making a measurable and material difference. To behave otherwise puts the growing CSR movement in jeopardy.

10

You: The Ultimate X-Factor

While writing this book, I've had the pleasure of having hundreds of conversations with people at all levels of organizations who are integrating purpose into their businesses and their careers. By design, the major focus of our conversations was on the business benefits they were seeing. But one topic was a big surprise and was spontaneously raised by more people than I would have imagined.

I remember one interview with the marketing director of a start-up focused on healthy food and beverages. We had met on the sidelines of a conference in Aspen, Colorado. When I told him the concept for this book, he got excited and immediately began to recount for me all the ways his company had embedded purpose into their business model. Their focus was healthy foods focused on kids, at prices significantly lower than incumbents like Whole Foods. The goal was to assure that "It's not only rich people who can afford to feed their children in the right way." He was particularly excited that their sales force could use their mission to connect with and inspire their potential customers. He was also proud to have a small group of angel investors who wanted a fair return on their investment but were willing to sacrifice a bit of that to "always do the right thing."

As we ran over our allotted thirty minutes, he pointed at my iPhone and said, "Can we shut the recording off for a moment?"

I immediately complied, secretly hoping that I was going to get some off-the-record scoop. He smiled and took a long deep breath of the cool Rocky Mountain air. "Look, I think it's important to tell you this. I know in my head that all these salient business points are important, and that that's the focus of your book. But I also need to tell you that even if there were not all these benefits, we would still do what we're doing. Supporting local farmers makes me feel better about my role in our community, and having an eco-friendly supply chain means we're doing something about global warming. Looking out for stray dogs is important to a lot of our employees. And to my kids— they love talking about dogs! So, while I'm happy telling you about all the business benefits we see from running our company with a deeply embedded mission, the reality is that those are simply the icing on the cake. I'd be doing all of this regardless, because it makes every day leading my company a happier and more meaningful day."

The Case for You!

The majority of this book has tried to make a case for businesses to integrate a sense of purpose into their DNA. I close by positing that there's an even more important reason for purpose: *you!*

You count. You matter. You get a vote—the deciding one, in fact!

The only person who ultimately owns your career choices is you— not your boss, not your board, not those skeptics who might try to talk you out of it. And the great news for you—and for the world—is that there are more choices and opportunities out there than ever before.

You get to decide whether you're going to embrace business as usual and have *work* remain a four-letter word, or if instead you will join the migration and use the power of capitalism to be a force for good in our world. And I believe that if you take on that challenge (or dial it up even further compared to what you're currently doing), the ultimate beneficiaries will not just be your business and society—but also you and your family.

Think back to the last Good Samaritan deed you did. How did it make you feel? Maybe you brought food to an elderly shut-in or left the bus one stop early to chase down a fellow passenger who left her purse behind. Remember how that made you feel a glow that changed your day?

Now remember that moment of generosity—when it was you at your very best—and imagine if moments like this were part of each workday. What if doing good for your community and the world was written into your job description?

Business: The Next Generation

Aaron Michel grew up with his sights set on being a hotshot lawyer. It was all he wanted to do, and he had the whole road mapped out. On the eve of matriculating to law school, Michel decided that perhaps he should try a corporate-law internship before committing all that time and money to the cause, and within a week, he knew that the legal world wasn't for him.

"I suddenly realized that I needed to figure out a way to combine my professional interests with a greater purpose," he says. He quickly changed tracks—attending Harvard Business School instead—and the now-happy CEO still marvels at "how close [he] got to spending [his] life in the wrong field." This course correction, this lucky pivot, is the inspiration behind Michel's Bay Area startup PathSource, a web and mobile career-navigation technology.

PathSource's mission is to empower young adults to make smarter decisions about their future. The platform has a deep bench of useful tools: there's a career recommendation engine; an inventory of different college-admission requirements, specialties, and financial-aid opportunities; a video library with almost three thousand informational interviews with professionals; an active job-listings board; even a survey to determine how much income one needs to earn to support himself or herself. "We try to connect the dots between education, career, lifestyle, and budget," says Michel. "We want young people to understand the pipeline between the decisions they make today and their lives ten years from now."

PathSource's timing couldn't be better. The United States is in the middle of a serious national conversation about the country's educational system. Is college for everyone? Are there alternate pathways to the middle class? Should the government subsidize student debt? How can we better prepare young adults for the twenty-first-century job market? These are the questions we ask in response to alarming figures that show education is not making good on its promise. More than half of college graduates seeking jobs did not have an offer by graduation, and 44 percent of college graduates are employed in jobs that don't require a college degree.[69]

Dig a bit deeper and you'll find a trail of similarly frustrating stats: in high schools across the country, there is an average of 859 students per college counselor, and college career centers are chronically underfunded, with a median operating budget of less than $34,000. With student debt at a record high of $1.1 trillion, and almost 20 percent of student borrowers in default, education is at risk of becoming an institution as likely to enslave as it is to serve. PathSource steps into this so-called crisis, eager to strengthen the connection between education and jobs—and to return power to the people.

Michel is a man of refreshing candor, particularly in an industry known for rewarding swagger, and he takes pains to point out that despite PathSource's current momentum, "this was hardly an overnight success." There was the usual buffet of #startupproblems—domain wars, disappearing profit streams, misguided sales pitches to people with no decision-making power. But his deep belief that he could have a positive impact and that all of this was a means to a purposeful end kept him motivated.

Today PathSource is an undeniable success. It's been featured as one of the twenty "Best New Apps" in the Apple App Store, and it ranks as the number-one most popular career and professional app in the education category. It has experienced 650 percent growth in daily downloads since its launch in January, and an initial round of fundraising raised $1.4 million from investors like Ironfire Capital and Wasabi Ventures. Education partners include the San Francisco Unified School District and Chicago Public Schools and more than twenty universities like MIT, Northeastern, and Boston University. The dream of every consumer brand is to build a product that users don't just like but *love*. PathSource's 4.85-out-of-5-star rating across more than 4,400 ratings indicate it has achieved that rare status.

But Aaron says that's not even the best part. "I wake up every morning excited to read our users' reviews. Not because I want to pull them for my next pitch deck, but because hearing their stories makes me feel like my workdays count for something. That the long hours are worth it. That this career is worth it."

For the Next Twenty Minutes...

Please don't think about business. At all.

Instead, allow me to close this book with a pivot. I'm going to posit that not every reason to do something in business and your career must be based upon the bottom line. And there's no reason to feel guilty about that.

I've argued against false dichotomies, such as the canard that purpose is antithetical to profits. I'm now going to take on another one: that something that is good for you personally must somehow be bad for business. The simple fact is that purpose can be good for a company's profitability, longevity and enterprise value, while also being great for you—mentally, physically, and spiritually.

So, for the next twenty minutes, please get comfortable, then get a bit self-centered, as we're only going to be talking about *you*.

"The Disease Is the Enemy"

Do you ever have one of those mornings when you just can't get excited to get out of bed and begin that slog to work? Or have you stared in annoyance at the online boarding pass that just *dinged* on your phone as you thought, "The last bloody thing I want to do right now is get on another plane"? Of course you have—it happens to the best of us, and yet somehow, we must suck it up and "turn that frown upside down."

How much better off would we be psychologically if we deeply believed that our company was making a real difference in the world? Would that increase your motivation? I was asked about this after a speech in London. At dinner, one of the attendees shared her existential *angst* with the table: "I used to think I had the dream job. But now I realize I'm just trying to slug it out for one more point of market share for…toothpaste! Toothpaste! I mean, seriously, I've spent the last six months fighting for more shelf space in two large retailers. Even if we succeed, that just means that Crest picks up a tenth of a market-share point from Colgate. *That* is why I'm supposed to wake up motivated every morning?"

She then asked the table whether we could cite examples of leaders we'd met who could inspire people in such a way that they psychologically viewed their career as a "true positive" in their lives.

When it was my turn, I recollected my experiences talking with employees at every level of Edwards Lifesciences, and how they always seemed so motivated to "give our patients a second chance to live their entire life." I brought up my interview with their CEO, Mike Mussallem, and how I had asked him whether he thought the firm's purpose gave it an advantage over competitors when it came to recruiting top talent.

He started by challenging my question (thankfully in a nonaggressive manner): "You asked about competition, but I need to clarify that. When you're purpose driven in the way we are, you don't put all your energy into beating a competitor. I've been in that type of environment—we all have. But here in this company, we make the problems our patients have our enemy. *We make the disease the enemy*, rather than other companies in our field. And when you can reduce that to language and messages for your employees, and they understand it, then that's how we *win*. It elevates our game."

Wow! Wake up hungry to go fight the issues that kill patients and take them away from their families. I don't know about you, but I'd happily run onto *that* playing field any day of the week.

Psychological Well-Being

The psychic well-being you feel as you fight a disease, tutor inner-city kids, or bring clean water to African villages is one manifestation of how a sense of purpose can affect your mental well-being, your health, and even your longevity. I'm happy to report that purpose can make you physically healthier. Not like a "miracle diet pill" advertised in one of those annoying pop-up ads or late-night infomercials, but real and scientifically proven health benefits.

In the United States, people who reported having a sense of purpose spend an average of 17 percent less time in hospitals. They're also more likely to make greater use of preventive care. After all, if you feel like you have a reason to stick around and that people need you,

you're much more likely to think about the long-term implications of the daily decisions you make—on diet, exercise, smoking, alcohol consumption, and others.

A 2014 study published in the *Lancet* found that people over age sixty-five who had a higher personal sense of purpose and well-being were more likely to live longer. The study followed nine thousand people over nearly a decade. And it turns out that lack of purpose late in life can end your life early! The study revealed that for those who rated themselves in the lowest category for having purpose in their life, 29 percent died during the study period. Their instance of mortality was over three times those who ranked highest on the purpose scale (only 9 percent of whom died).

Purpose Does a Body Good

According to the Centers for Disease Control and Prevention, the essential components of positive mental health include optimism, hopefulness, purpose in life, control of one's environment, spirituality, self-direction, and positive relationships.[70] Stop for a moment and review, item by item, how many of those boxes are ticked if you feel that each day at work is one with an embedded sense of purpose.

The benefits of living purposefully even include ones you might never have imagined. For example, research conducted at the Rush University Medical Center in Chicago suggests a strong sense of purpose can protect the brain.

Participants in Rush's Memory and Aging Project agree to yearly testing while alive and to then donate their organs upon death so that their brain tissue can be examined. Four different studies published by the research team confirmed the benefits of having a life filled with purpose. The test subjects who scored higher on the purpose scale were:

- 29 percent less likely to develop mild cognitive impairment;

- 52 percent less likely to develop Alzheimer's disease;
- 44 percent less likely to have a stroke; and
- two and a half times more likely to be free of dementia.

"Purpose somehow gives your brain resilience," says Patricia A. Boyle, PhD, a neuropsychologist with the Rush Alzheimer's Disease Center. "It makes your brain stronger and more resistant to the effects of diseases like Alzheimer's."

The Happiness Principle

Would you prefer to live in a sad country or a happy one? Almost everyone (other than novelists named Sartre) would of course choose the latter. To help you find the happiest countries, there's a handy guide. Every year the Sustainable Development Solutions Network, an international panel of social scientists convened by the United Nations, releases its World Happiness Report. The rankings are based on a simple life-evaluation tool that asks people around the world:

"Please imagine a ladder, with steps numbered from 0 at the bottom to 10 at the top. The top of the ladder represents the best possible life for you and the bottom of the ladder represents the worst possible life for you. On which step of the ladder would you say you personally feel you stand at this time?"[71]

For 2017, the happiest countries were way higher on the ladder than the saddest. The top five nations averaged a score of 7.5, while the five saddest were at 3.2.

So, who tops the list? Norway, Denmark, Iceland, Switzerland, and Finland. My own country, the United States, came in at fourteen. Since nobody wants to chant, "We're number fourteen! We're number fourteen!" I read the full study and was very interested to see that purpose plays a role in national happiness.

The study determined that three-quarters of the variation among countries can be attributed to six underlying variables: income per capita, healthy life expectancy, social support, freedom to make life choices, perceived corruption of government and business, and…drumroll…generosity of donations.

Why were Americans less happy in 2016? It was not due to per capita income—that had increased. It was not because of health or life expectancy—both were moving in a positive direction. One of the study's editors, Dr. Jeffrey Sachs, explained, "We're getting richer, but our social capital is deteriorating."[72] Social support, perceived personal freedom, trust in government and business, and lack of generosity all contribute to a "happiness" crisis in America.

So, nations that have a sense of purpose and generosity also have higher overall happiness. What is true in our personal lives has been statistically proven to be true at both a national and a global level.

The phenomenon of people with purpose being healthier and happier is not confined to just the United States. Let's look at the nation most successful at healthy aging: Japan. Few places on earth can promise the average citizen a longer life. Today, Japanese women who reach age sixty-five can expect to live an additional twenty-three years—until age eighty-eight! Men who reach sixty-five will have on average an additional eighteen years.[73]

Many factors have been cited for this long life expectancy, including a low-fat diet, healthy quantities of fish and rice, and a strong social safety net. But did you know that studies in Japan have also found a link between purpose and longevity?

According to Yoshiko Matsumoto, a linguistics professor at Stanford University and the author of *Faces of Aging: The Lived Experiences of the Elderly in Japan*, the transition to retirement often includes a reevaluation of life's purpose, along with one's identity and social role. "Older people in Japan seek to be useful," Matsumoto said. "But they base their idea of being useful on their life purpose, or *ikigai*."[74]

Ikigai is the belief that your life is worth living. It includes purpose and meaning and has been translated by some as meaning "a reason for being" or "purpose in life." According to Matsumoto, *ikigai* guides "what people do each day, from exercise to social engagement to productive contributions and engagement with their families and society."[75]

A research study performed by Tohoku University Graduate School of Medicine in Sendai, Japan, bore this out. In a seven-year longitudinal study of over forty-three thousand Japanese adults, these researchers found that individuals who believed that their life was worth living were less likely to die than were their counterparts without this belief.

At the beginning of the study, almost 60 percent of the research participants reported a sense of *ikigai*. Those who did were more likely to be married, educated, and employed. They also reported lower levels of stress and better self-rated health. The study found, after controlling for all other variables, that *ikigai* predicted who was still alive after seven years. Ninety-five percent of the study participants who reported a sense of meaning in their lives were alive seven years after the initial survey, compared to 83 percent of those who reported no sense of meaning in their lives. The lack of *ikigai* was associated with death due to cardiovascular disease—usually stroke.

Purpose and Resilience

As I pitch up in various cities around the world to fly the Room to Read flag, people often ask me, "How do you do it? You're constantly on airplanes, landing in time zones far away from home, making speech after speech, and yet your energy level never seems to flag." My reply is consistent: I'm not sure how it would be possible for my energy level to be low. After all, I think I have one of the greatest jobs in the world, one that marries my passion for education and kids with the "inner entrepreneur" who lives to help build great organizations. So the high energy just comes naturally, and as a result I'm much more resilient.

I heard something similar from Vicky Tsai, the cofounder of Tatcha. When we first met over coffee in Hong Kong, it was she who was just off a plane, but she looked like she was winning the war against jet lag. When I asked her to tell me more about their "Beautiful Faces, Beautiful Futures" campaign, she talked first about the trip she had made to Cambodia to meet a group of twenty young women whose education was being aided by her company. But next, just like the food and beverage entrepreneur I'd interviewed in Aspen, she said the impact was not just being felt by the young women in our program but deeply impacted her personally:

> Let me be clear—our company is not yet profitable, and several parts of my car are being held together with duct tape. But I would never give up this program, because it's not only what the world needs, it's also the reason I get out of bed in the morning. Being a start-up is tough—you're always fighting brush fires, there's always some obstacle you had not expected to face, and you work extreme hours because your staffing is lean. But every morning I remind myself that we must get more distribution, expand our line, and sell more product, or else we will let so many girls down. This gives me the energy to push hard and the resilience to get back up again on those inevitable days when I get knocked down.

My Family Was Very Proud

As I talked to more people like Vicky about having purpose baked into their day-to-day work, I thought again about John German, the man who brought down Volkswagen. How did it feel, I asked, to know that you not only stood up for what was right but also sent a message that companies that do what VW did will pay a very heavy price? To have sent one of the most powerful environmental messages of the last decade to big business? Here's his response:

I've always had mixed feelings about this. I have friends that work at VW, including the engineer who finally admitted to CARB that VW was using defeat devices (against his orders). And the industry doesn't need another black eye.

But cheating undermines the entire industry, as it puts companies that want to do the right thing at a competitive disadvantage, creating a race to the bottom. This is clearly seen in Europe, where all manufacturers have diesel vehicles with high emissions (although BMW does seem to be a bit better than the rest). It is extremely important to make sure the same thing does not happen in the US. VW's actions were particularly egregious because of the way that they lied to the agencies for sixteen months—they richly deserve everything they got.

I am humbled to have been a part of this, but the real credit goes to EPA and CARB for having created effective enforcement systems and to the 1970 Clean Air Act for giving the agencies the authority to create these effective systems.

And how, I asked him, did your family feel?

"My family was very proud. Many of them followed the articles, radio, and TV interviews with great interest. My wife thinks I have been underappreciated in my career, and she sees this as something to which I am due."

The Dinner-Table Conversation

I heard a similar story from Scott Ullem of Edwards Lifesciences, who once told me that the best part of his job switch was what happened at the end of the day. "This job has totally changed the nature of our dinner-table conversations. During my old days as a banker or CFO of a plastics company, what could I talk to them about? M&A? EPS? That really cool revision I had made to our statement of cash flows? But now it's different—we talk about patients I've met or what they experienced when they toured the production facility where the heart valves are sewn."

During a follow-up conversation over email, I asked Scott about the specific reactions his three children (aged nine to fifteen) had. He copied his fifteen-year-old daughter, Caroline, in on his response and asked her to tell me in her own words, while also giving her a free pass: "It's okay if your answer is, 'I wish he would stop talking so I can finish dinner and go back to studying.'"

By the following morning, I had received her response:

My dad loves to talk about his work during family time and dinner. This isn't because he has earned a lot of money or has a prestigious position, but because he finds true passion in the work that he does. This teaches me and my brothers that success is not found in how much money you make or other material results, but in the joy you find in the work you do. I really appreciate hearing this message because it is so easy in environments like high school to get caught up in the final product of your hard work like what college you're going to get into, or whether you'll eventually have a high paying job. My dad's love of his work teaches me that the joy found in the journey to success (of perseverance and grit) is just as valuable as the result of the hard work. This makes me much more motivated to pursue interests that bring me joy.

Best of all, Caroline was not just passively watching her father's example. Caroline's note did not stop after talking about her father. She also proudly reported that she had recently taken on leadership of a book drive in her school to collect books for their local women's and children's shelter, and on weekends she was an instructor for special-needs skiers.

Could anything make parents more proud than seeing purpose become a family sport?

Reasons to Believe

I'm optimistic that every one of us can move his or her career and life to a place that is more purpose driven. There are many reasons for this belief:

More career options than ever: When I told my food-obsessed wife, Amy, about the rapid growth of Revolution Foods, her response was: "There are so many cool companies out there these days. When I was in high school, the guidance counselors never told us how many great options we had." There are, of course, more by the day, as traditional companies begin to embrace purpose and as more and more B Corps get launched. At the time of this writing, there are over twenty-two hundred of them, in over fifty countries, working across 130 industries.

Build your own: If you're purpose driven but can't find the right job or the right company, take heart! It's never been easier or cheaper to start your own firm. Vicky Tsai told me, "I had become disenchanted not so much with the corporate world but rather with my place in it. I had come to the realization that I needed to believe in something more than just making money for myself or just selling coffee or whatever I'm selling that day to be motivated. It can be so demoralizing to work so hard and not have something bigger that you're working towards." So, she started her own company and every day has the satisfaction of helping more girls across the developing world go to school.

Follow-the-leader: Starting a company is not for everyone, and fortunately playing follow-the-leader can also be an effective way to inculcate purpose into your work. Pick a few leaders you admire (be they Elon Musk, Wendy Kopp of Teach for America, or Mark Tercek at the Nature Conservancy) or companies who inspire (Lyft, Edwards Lifesciences, Kickstarter, or Etsy) and then go make the case to their HR departments that they'd be foolish not to hire a talented and purpose-driven person like you.

Age is no barrier: Back in the old days, young people used to be advised to break their lives into three sequential parts: learn, earn, return. That may have made sense at the time, but if doing good for your community and the world brings a deep sense of satisfaction, then why wait until you're old to enjoy that glow? Remember Matt

Dee, who turned down Snapchat to work for Oscar, as a millennial poster child, and Scott Ullem, who made the switch at age forty-seven and happily reports that "there's no going back!"

Purpose transcends hierarchy: Some of the best purpose-driven innovations come from the front lines. Caryn Freiberger was a VP on the Foreign Exchange Institutional Sales Desk at Citibank when she and the FX management team proposed the idea of an "e for Education" initiative and then sold it up the food chain. The idea was that each time a client chose to do a foreign-exchange transaction on Citi's Velocity platform, the firm would make a microdonation to a basket of education charities that had passed Citi's due-diligence process. Five years later, she can proudly report that over $22 million has been gifted to seven education nonprofits—proving that you don't have to be in the C-suite to have a huge effect on connecting cause to capitalism.

Old guard or new, both work: Integrating purpose into your company can look as shiny and high tech as Tesla or as old-school and unglamorous as Raven Hydraulic Supply—or anywhere in between. The food industry, as an example, sits in the middle of this spectrum. As one of WhiteWave's HR executives told me, "People want to work at WhiteWave Foods because we're creating the kind of company that we can all be proud of, a place where we work to be the kind of change we want to see in the world."

Purpose does not make you poor: The truth of the modern world is that purpose does not equal an express lane to the poorhouse. You don't have to be Mother Teresa, or Gandhi sleeping on the bare floor in his only robe. Maybe you turn into Marc Benioff or the Atlassian cofounders. Or maybe you join a similar company when it's young and growing. You might devise a portfolio career, with half focused on making a difference and half focused on making a salary. Maybe you emulate my example and learn to live with a smaller paycheck but a bigger heart.

The End-of-Life View

For over a decade I've worked with a Vancouver-based executive coach named Jeff Balin. Jeff is a Kellogg MBA who cut his teeth in the Starbucks management-training program while at the same time studying Tibetan Buddhism, Judaism, and other spiritual sources. I once asked him if he had ever pondered the secret to life. He paused thoughtfully and replied, "The secret to life? For that, you need to look to the teachings of the great spiritual traditions."

"OK. But what if one's life is frantic, and he doesn't have time to do all that reading—but luckily, he's talking to a guy who has? Can you save me some time and give me the keys to the kingdom?"

Jeff breathed deeply—I think because my request went against our usual Socratic dialogue. "Many of the teachings would suggest that we should do one simple thing. Just one. Figure out what you want to say on your deathbed, and work backwards from there."

He paused to let it sink in. "If what you want to say on your final day is in alignment with how you're currently living your life, then stop navel gazing, and just get back to living. But if you're not in alignment, then you'd better start making some adjustments before much more of life passes you by."

Do you know what *you* want to say as you sit on that porch swing and look back on your life? Is your current life in alignment with that? And can purpose play a role?

A Better World, a Better You

I've made the case earlier as to why I think purpose can be a win-win-win. It can help to create much better businesses, while making the world and your community a better place. It's with great optimism that I'm writing about this third win—a better life for *you*.

I've been blessed in my post-Microsoft life to wake up every morning excited and hugely motivated for the day ahead. I know that my work matters, and I remind myself that what I accomplish will have significance to so many millions of children who did not get the lucky breaks in life that I did. Even little quotidian tasks like expense reports and reading board minutes are put in perspective—they're all a means to an end, and for me that end is more education for more kids in more places.

I want that same feeling to be part of everyday life for you, the reader. Over thirty years into my own career, I see the vast difference between those I meet who have lives and careers imbued with purpose and those who are just slogging through another day. Recall the Gallup study cited in chapter 3, in which 70 percent of employees said they don't feel engaged at work. If you're part of that group, then perhaps this chapter will serve as a permission slip to begin to envision an alternative future.

As one friend said to me, "The world has more than enough crappy companies. Why should I spend my precious time helping to create one more?" A different view emerged when I asked Seth Godin to name a company he deeply respected. "To me, Patagonia is the magic story. Not because they have maximized profits (they haven't— no way, no how) but because they make *enough*. And enough is enough, especially when you get to be a good human."

I've had the pleasure of meeting hundreds of people who have crossed this chasm, and they always seem like the happiest and most well-adjusted people in the world. I hope that you will join them in this powerful movement. How will you feel if you jump out of bed eager to go to work on Monday morning? Or to walk into the office with a broad smile on your face and a spring in your step? Can you imagine how much fun you'll have, and how proud you'll feel, as you tell your friends over lunch about the clean water well you helped bring to a rural village in Kenya? To share photos with your Facebook friends of smiling families in front of the new homes built with your support of Habitat for Humanity?

What would you like to tell your family around the dinner table about your day at the office? How will it feel if, like in Vicky Tsai's household, your daughter is reporting on the balance of funds held in her elephant bank to fund girls' scholarships? At your next university reunion, do you want to play that annoying one-upmanship game where your classmates compare where they are on the org chart, or do you want to steer the conversation to something more meaningful?

Together, we can link cause with capitalism in a way that changes the future and forever answers the question of whether business can be a force for good. To repeat a phrase from earlier, you were not born merely to make money. Our lives and our careers are a long road. And the road that is paved with purpose is the one that has a better view and that is much more fun to travel. I sincerely hope you'll join me on it—not just for the good of your company, but for your own happiness with life.

Notes

1. Ryan Honeyman, *The B Corp Handbook: How to Use Business as a Force for Good* (San Francisco: Berrett-Koehler Publishers, 2014).

2. Edelman, *Citizens Engage! Edelman Goodpurpose Study 2010: Fourth Annual Global Consumer Survey*, November 11, 2011, https://www.scribd.com/doc/72422362?secret_password=cxw357dw8arqe42e53s

3. "The One-for-One Business Model: Avoiding Unintended Consequences," *Knowledge at Wharton*, February 16, 2015, http://knowledge.wharton.upenn.edu/article/one-one-business-model-social-impact-avoiding-unintended-consequences/

4. "Is There a Serious Problem with Coffee Capsules?" *BBC News Magazine*, February 19, 2016, http://www.bbc.com/news/magazine-35605927

5. Ann Gynn, "Purpose-Driven Content Marketing: Brands That Give and Get," *Content Marketing Institute*, August 22, 2014, http://contentmarketinginstitute.com/2014/08/purpose-driven-content-marketing-brands/

6. Emmie Martin, "This Company Is Pulling in $125 Million in Sales by Cooking Up a Solution to Sad School Lunches," *Business Insider*, July 7, 2016, http://www.businessinsider.com/revolution-foods-changing-the-school-lunch-industry-2016-6

7. "Biting Commentary," *Economist*, May 4, 2013, http://www.economist.com/news/united-states/21577098-new-company-trying-make-school-meals-healthier-biting-commentary

8. Martin, "This Company Is Pulling in $125 Million in Sales."

9. Jessica Pothering, "How Revolution Foods Made a Business of Healthy Food for Healthier Students," *Entrepreneur*, October 14, 2014, https://www.entrepreneur.com/article/238277

10. "Biting Commentary."

11. Ibid.

12. Bruce Japsen, "Year after Cigarette Ban, CVS Says 95 Million Fewer Packs Sold at 'All Retailers,'" *Forbes*, September 3, 2015, https://www.forbes.com/sites/brucejapsen/2015/09/03/year-after-cvs-cigarette-ban-95-million-fewer-packs-sold-by-all-retailers/#26f0601d6835

13. Ibid.

14. Ibid.

15. Bob Al-Greene, "Thirty Overused Buzzwords in Digital Marketing," *Mashable*, May 23, 2013, http://mashable.com/2013/05/23/buzzword-infographic/

16. Farhad Manjoo, "How Battling Brands Online Has Gained Urgency, and Impact," *New York Times*, June 21, 2017, https://www.nytimes.com/2017/06/21/technology/how-battling-brands-online-has-gained-urgency-and-impact.html

17. Tara Parker-Pope, "How Parents Harnessed the Power of Social Media to Challenge EpiPen Prices," *New York Times*, August 25, 2016, https://well.blogs.nytimes.com/2016/08/25/how-parents-harnessed-the-power-of-social-media-to-challenge-epipen-prices/?_r=0

18. Frank Chung, "Shareholders Vote Down Mylan Chair's $128 Million Package," *News.com.au*, June 26 2017, http://www.news.com.au/finance/work/leaders/shareholders-vote-down-mylan-chairs-128-million-package/news-story/2b25a22b77131666c1d9be3cb48975b8

19. "Mylan Agrees to Settlement on Medicaid Rebate Classification for EpiPen Auto-Injector," *Mylan.com*, October 7, 2016, http://newsroom.mylan.com/2016-10-07-Mylan-Agrees-to-Settlement-on-Medicaid-Rebate-Classification-for-EpiPen-Auto-Injector

20. Christina Sterbenz, "The CEO of EpiPen Maker Mylan Once Claimed She Had an MBA That She Never Earned," *Business Insider*, August 25, 2016, http://www.businessinsider.com/mylan-ceo-heather-bresch-west-virginia-university-mba-scandal-2016-8

21. Robyn O'Brien, "Head of CVS Pharmacy, a Mother of Four Responds to EpiPen Pricing," *Robynobrien.com*, January 13, 2017, https://robynobrien.com/inside-cvs-a-mother-of-four-responds-to-epigate-concerns/

22. WestJetter, "When a Virus at Christmas Is a Good Thing: Real-Time Giving Video Goes Viral," *WestJet.com*, December 10, 2013, https://blog.westjet.com/westjet-christmas-miracle-video-goes-viral/

23. Kristina Monllos, "This Canadian Airline Wants You to Help It Complete 12,000 Miracles in Twenty-Four Hours," *Adweek*, December 9, 2015, http://www.adweek.com/brand-marketing/canadian-airline-wants-you-help-it-complete-12000-miracles-24-hours-168538/

24. Andrew Bender, "The Real 'Christmas Miracle' of WestJet's Viral Video: Millions in Free Advertising," *Forbes*, December 12, 2013, https://www.forbes.com/sites/andrewbender/2013/12/12/the-real-christmas-miracle-of-westjets-viral-video-millions-in-free-advertising/#20c701fb22be

25. Jenni Ryall, "The Secret to Atlassian, Australia's 'Best Place to Work,'" *Mashable*, September 3, 2015, http://mashable.com/2015/09/03/atlassian-best-place-work/

26. Ibid.

27. Rebecca Knight, "MBA Students Help Ethiopia Tackle the Impact of Urbanization," *Financial Times*, January 29, 2017, https://www.ft.com/content/f027d588-d9b3-11e6-944b-e7eb37a6aa8e?mhq5j=e5

28. Robert Safian, "Salesforce's Marc Benioff on the Power of Values," *Fast Company*, April 17, 2017, https://www.fastcompany.com/40397514/salesforces-marc-benioff-on-the-power-of-values

29. Martin, "This Company Is Pulling in $125 Million in Sales."

30. Ashlee Vance, Elon Musk: How the Billionaire CEO of SpaceX and Tesla Is Shaping Our Future (London: Virgin Books, 2016).

31. "Elon Musk Named Innovator of the Year in Technology by WSJ Magazine," *Tesla.com*, October 28, 2011, https://www.tesla.com/blog/elon-musk-named-innovator-year-technology-wsj-magazine

32. Vance, *Elon Musk*.

33. Ibid.

34. Gallup, *State of the American Workplace*, February 2017, http://news.gallup.com/reports/199961/7.aspx

35. "Talent Repelled by Unethical Business Practices, Says EY's Survey," *EY*, June 18, 2015, http://www.ey.com/us/en/newsroom/news-releases/news-talent-repelled-by-unethical-business-practices-says-eys-survey

36. Barry Schwartz, "Rethinking Work," *New York Times*, August 28, 2015, https://www.nytimes.com/2015/08/30/opinion/sunday/rethinking-work.html

37. Sarah K. Yazinski, "Strategies for Retaining Employees and Minimizing Turnover," *HR.BLR.com*, August 3, 2009, http://hr.blr.com/whitepapers/Staffing-Training/Employee-Turnover/Strategies-for-Retaining-Employees-and-Minimizing-

38. John Bersin, "Employee Retention Now a Big Issue: Why the Tide has Turned," *Linkedin.com*, August 16, 2013, https://www.linkedin.com/pulse/20130816200159-131079-employee-retention-now-a-big-issue-why-the-tide-has-turned

39. All statistics and quotes provided in author interview with the bank's corporate-citizenship team.

40. Emerging World, *2017 CISL Impact Benchmark Study*, 2017, http://www.emergingworld.com/documents//2017-cisl-study/2017-cisl-impact-benchmark-study-443.pdf; Emerging World, *2015 CISL Impact Benchmark Study*, 2015, http://www.emergingworld.com/documents/2015-cisl-impact-benchmark-study-289.pdf

41. "Intrapreneur," *Investopedia*, n.d., http://www.investopedia.com/terms/i/intrapreneur.asp

42. Quentin Hardy, "Marc Benioff, Salesforce Chief, on the Strategic Benefits of Corporate Giving," *New York Times*, November 2, 2015, https://www.nytimes.com/2015/11/08/giving/marc-benioff-salesforce-chief-on-the-strategic-benefits-of-corporate-giving.html

43. Safian, "Salesforce's Marc Benioff."

44. Matteo Gamba, "What Is Airbnb's Mission/Vision Statement?," *Quora*, April 21, 2016, https://www.quora.com/What-is-Airbnbs-mission-vision-statement

45. Brad Stone, The Upstarts: How Uber, Airbnb, and the Killer Companies of the New Silicon Valley Are Changing the World (New York: Little, Brown, 2017).

46. Shell, "Sandy's Impact: Opening Doors in a Time of Need," *Airbnb.com*, n.d., https://www.airbnb.com/community-stories/new-york/sandys-impact

47. Ibid.

48. Airbnb, "A New Helping Hand for Our Disaster-Response Program," *Airbnb.com*, June 29, 2015, https://blog.atairbnb.com/a-new-helping-hand-for-our-disaster-response-program/

49. Ibid.

50. "Denver Host Opens Her Home to Refugees," *Airbnb.com*, April 7, 2017, https://www.airbnbcitizen.com/denver-host-opens-home-refugees/

51. Jeffrey Sohl, "A Cautious Restructuring of the Angel Market in 2016 with a Robust Appetite for Seed and Start-Up Investing," *Center for Venture Research*, May 31, 2017, https://paulcollege.unh.edu/sites/paulcollege.unh.edu/files/cvr-reports/2016AnalysisReportFinal_0.pdf

52. Personal conversation with author, 2009.

53. Jessica Harris, "Ethics in a Bottle," *CNN.com*, November 5, 2007, http://money.cnn.com/2007/10/31/smbusiness/Ethos.fsb/index.htm

54. Ibid.

55. Ibid.

56. Ibid.

57. "Ethos Water Fund," *Starbucks.com*, n.d., http://www.starbucks.com/responsibility/community/ethos-water-fund

58. "What You Need to Know about Impact Investing," *Global Impact Investing Network*, n.d., https://thegiin.org/impact-investing/need-to-know/

59. Sarah Murray, "Investing for Good: The Rich History and the Bright Future of Impact Investing," *B the Change*, December 5, 2016, https://bthechange.com/investing-for-good-6423fcff91a6

60. Ibid.

61. *2014 US Trust Insights on Wealth and Worth Survey: Key Findings* (n.p.: US Trust, 2014), http://www.ustrust.com/publish/content/application/pdf/GWMOL/USTp_AR4GWF53F_2015-06.pdf

62. Marta Maretich, "Women Rule: Why the Future of Social, Sustainable, and Impact Investing Is in Female Hands," *Maximpact Blog*, n.d., http://maximpactblog.com/women-rule-why-the-future-of-social-sustainable-and-impact-investing-is-in-female-hands/

63. "The Regulatory Cost of Being JPMorgan," *Financial Times*, January 10, 2014, https://www.ft.com/content/a1b6bb7c-79ed-11e3-a3e6-00144feabdc0

64. Adi Ignatius and Daniel McGinn, "Novo Nordisk CEO Lars Sørensen on What Propelled Him to the Top," *Harvard Business Review*, November 2015, https://hbr.org/2015/11/novo-nordisk-ceo-on-what-propelled-him-to-the-top

65. "Fraud and Abuse Online: Harmful Practices in Internet Payday Lending," *Pewtrusts.org*, October 2, 2014, http://www.pewtrusts.org/en/research-and-analysis/reports/2014/10/fraud-and-abuse-online-harmful-practices-in-internet-payday-lending

66. Susan Tompor, "Google's Ad Ban Puts Payday Lenders on the Defensive," *USA Today*, May 29, 2016, http://www.usatoday.com/story/money/personalfinance/2016/05/29/googles-ad-ban-puts-payday-lenders-defensive/84992818/

67. Michael Corkery, "As Coal's Future Grows Murkier, Banks Pull Financing," *New York Times*, March 20, 2016, https://www.nytimes.com/2016/03/21/business/dealbook/as-coals-future-grows-murkier-banks-pull-financing.html?_r=0

68. Ibid.

69. Ibid.

70. "Cathay Pacific Reports HK$6b Earnings, Passenger and Cargo Revenue Falls," *Standard* (Hong Kong), March 9, 2016, http://www.thestandard.com.hk/breaking-news.php?id=72272

71. Danny Lee, "Cathay Pacific Targeted in Shark-Fin Protest at Hong Kong International Airport," *South China Morning Post*, May 30, 2016, http://www.scmp.com/news/hong-kong/health-environment/article/1958732/cathay-pacific-targeted-shark-fin-protest-hong

72. Robert Lee Hotz, "As World Crowds In, Cities Become Digital Laboratories," *Wall Street Journal*, December 11, 2015, https://www.wsj.com/articles/as-world-crowds-in-cities-become-digital-laboratories-1449850244

73. Ibid.

74. Andrew Winston, "What VW Didn't Understand about Trust," *Harvard Business Review*, September 23, 2015, https://hbr.org/2015/09/what-vw-didnt-understand-about-trust

75. Jan Schwartz and Victoria Bryan, "VW's Dieselgate Bill Hits $30 Bln After Another Charge," *Reuters*, September 29, 2017, http://www.reuters.com/article/legal-uk-volkswagen-emissions/vws-dieselgate-bill-hits-30-bln-after-another-charge-idUSKCN1C4271

76. David Gelles, "Social Responsibility That Rubs Right Off," *New York Times*, October 17, 2015, https://www.nytimes.com/2015/10/18/business/energy-environment/social-responsibility-that-rubs-right-off.html

77. "Introduction to Stopgreenwash.org," *Stopgreenwash.org*, n.d., http://www.stopgreenwash.org/introduction

78. Kristina Monllos, "How Pepsi Got It So Wrong: Unpacking One of the Most Reviled Ads in Recent Memory," *Adweek*, April 5, 2017, http://www.adweek.com/brand-marketing/how-pepsi-got-it-so-wrong-unpacking-one-of-the-most-reviled-ads-in-recent-memory/

79. Daniel Kleinman, "Will Volkswagen's Possible $18 Billion Emissions Penalty Drive Transparency in Manufacturing?," *Forbes*, January 25, 2016, https://www.forbes.com/sites/danielkleinman/2016/01/25/will-volkswagens-possible-18-billion-emissions-penalty-drive-transparency-in-manufacturing/2/#49b431d34169

80. "The Labor Market for Recent College Graduates," *Newyorkfed.org*, n.d., https://www.newyorkfed.org/research/college-labor-market/index.html

81. Centers for Disease Control and Prevention, "Mental Health Basics," *CDC.gov*, October 4, 2013, https://www.cdc.gov/mentalhealth/basics.htm

82. Niraj Chokshi, "Norway Is No. 1 in Happiness. The United States, Sadly, Is No. 14," *New York Times*, March 20, 2017, https://www.nytimes.com/2017/03/20/world/worlds-happiest-countries.html

83. Ibid.

84. Dawn Carr, "Embracing the Japanese Approach to Aging," *Next Avenue*, May 22, 2013, http://www.nextavenue.org/why-we-need-embrace-japanese-approach-aging/

85. Ibid.

86. Ibid.

Acknowledgments

Writing a book is an exercise combining introversion, short bursts of insanely great productivity, and intense self-doubt. Twice now I have finished manuscripts with the words "never again," only to later abandon that vow. So here I am again.

The entire concept of this book came from Amalia, who originally suggested we cowrite a speech for corporate conferences on the subject. The book is written in first person for the sake of narrative simplicity, but it is a team effort. Amalia is an unparalleled brainstorming partner, an enthusiast, and a generator of the most inspiring turns of phrase. I hope this is not the only book we write together!

When I shared the initial speech concept with my good friend Ben Happ for his feedback, his immediate response was "Yes, but...this should also be your next book." As I warmed to the idea, I booked coffee in New York's East Village with the legendary author Seth Godin. His immediate response was, "You need to do this, and I will help in any way that I can." Thank you, Seth, for always being willing to challenge our thinking, believing in us, and encouraging us to never be complacent.

I'm thrilled to have worked again with Herb Schaffner, one of the best editors in the business. Herb and I originally met when he was with HarperCollins, and he guided this nervous first-time author as I wrote *Leaving Microsoft to Change the World*. It was chosen as one of Amazon's top ten business narratives of 2006, so to Herb I say, "Ahem...no pressure." Thank you also to Kristen Haff for her remarkable imagination, skill, and persistence in designing the book cover, and to Chloë Greene for making the words you're reading right now so beautiful on the page.

As this book began to come together, I tested out the potential content in front of several live audiences. Special thanks for those convenings to Connie Chue and the Kellogg Alumni Club of Hong Kong, Matthew Gollop of the Connected Group, NiQ Lai and the team at Hong Kong Broadband Networks, and Jolleen Jaworski and her monthly breakfast meetings of BCA Philadelphia.

Many early readers provided invaluable commentary as the manuscript came together (and sometimes fell apart). My gratitude to Jeff Balin, Amy Batchelor, Saniya Bloomer, Rebecca Brosnan, Tim Caflisch, CY Chang, Claire Diaz-Ortiz, Glenn Embrey, Patricia Horgan, Chris Jones, John Keith, Jaideep Khanna, Martina Lauchengco, Sonya Madden, Robert Menna, Eric Olsen, Sital Rupareila, Marshall Roslyn, Divya Samatani, Howard Temkin, Graves Tompkins, and Yusuf Alireza.

So many hyperbusy people were generous with their time as we peppered them with questions, interview requests, and more questions. This book would not have been possible without the positive and helpful spirit shown by Sarah Arblaster, Nick Adamus, Anne Black, Ashley Bouchard, Mike Cannon-Brooks, Gina Codd, Edith Cooper, Brian DeJaegher, Suzanne DiBianca, Matt Dee, Shelly Dee, Magda Donia, Marisa Drew, Scott Farquhar, Brad Feld, Daniel Freeman, Louis Gave,

Jonathan Greenblatt, Eva Halper, Laura Hemrika, Darcy Keller, Sanjana Khoobchandani, NiQ Lai, Sarah Levine, Zach Mercurio, Aaron Michel, Diane Mollenkopf, Geetha Murali, Mike Mussallem, Brad Murray, Frank O'Donnell, Eric Raynaud, John Ridding, Chris Sacca, Michael Schrage, Andrina Schwartz, Deborah Small, Brian Smith, Jessica Stacey, Nolan Taira, Michael Thatcher, Eric S. Thomas, Vicky Tsai, Caroline Ullem, Scott Ullem, Zoltan Varga, and Eze Vidra.

Amalia would like to send a special shout-out to her nearest and dearest: Mom, Dad, Robert, Howie, Chloe, Celia, Ben, Grammy, Grandfather, Grammums, and Gramps. And to her wonderful husband, Florian, she says, "Thank you for being such a smart, insightful first editor, for all those brainstorming sessions over dinner, for your insistence that I could do this and that it was worth doing, and for sometimes just offering me the hug I needed at the end of the day. I would never have come so far without you by my side.

"And to John, for his prolific pen, his unyielding positivity, his vision, and his grit. I'd hitch my wagon to just about anything you proposed!"

The person most responsible for getting me through the rough patches was my beautiful, smart, and loving wife, Amy. Every time I was in doubt, she would buck me up by saying things like, "The world needs for this book to be written, and you're the person to write it." With that, I "turned my frown upside down" and got back to work. Thank you, Ames, for being my partner in every aspect of our very full and exciting lives together.

I'm also very grateful that every morning I get to wake up and work alongside the best team in the business—my colleagues at Room to Read. The little-known and cash-strapped NGO that started in my second bedroom in 2000 has grown way beyond the wildest dreams of myself and my cofounders, Dinesh Shrestha and Erin Ganju. Thank you to them, our worldwide staff of fifteen hundred, our more than ten thousand volunteers in over fifty cities, and our global boards.

A final tip of the hat to my parents, Carolyn and Woody; my in-laws, Jan and Dave; and my sister, Lisa. All five have been constant inspiration on the most important thing we can learn from our elders: to vow every morning to live the best life we can possibly live.

Publishing With a Purpose

In support of Room to Read's work to bring the lifelong gift of education to millions of children around the world, John is donating his author profits to the organization. And you, dear reader, get to play a role in how those funds are deployed.

Our goal is to open at least ten new libraries serving over 4,000 children in low-income countries like Cambodia, Laos, Nepal and Vietnam. As a reader of this book, you'll be given the opportunity to vote on which country we open each library in. But wait, there's more! Readers will also be invited to attend the opening ceremony, with John, to cut the red ribbon and to meet the eager young readers whose lives will be forever changed.

—

To take part, please be sure to follow us on Twitter @PurposeIncBook.

About the Authors

Amalia McGibbon works for Social Good & Goodwill at Facebook. She's also a freelance food and travel writer, an avid photographer, and the author of the Amazon bestseller *The Choice Effect*. She lives in San Francisco with her husband, Florian Reichling.

John Wood is the founder of Room to Read and the author of *Leaving Microsoft to Change the World*. Named as one of the top ten business narratives of 2006 by Amazon and a top-ten nonfiction title by Hudson Books, the memoir was published in twenty-two languages. John was named by Goldman Sachs as one of the world's one hundred most intriguing entrepreneurs. He is a Henry Crown Fellow at the Aspen Institute and a Young Global Leader of the World Economic Forum, and he was awarded Microsoft's Alumni of the Year award by Bill and Melinda Gates. At the invitation of Bill Clinton, he served four terms on the advisory board of the Clinton Global Initiative. John lives in Hong Kong with his wife, Amy Powell. His hobbies include trail running, hiking, skiing, reading, and wine.

Also by Amalia McGibbon

The Choice Effect

—

Also by John Wood

Leaving Microsoft to Change the World

Creating Room to Read: A Story of Hope in the Battle for Global Literacy

Books for Kids

Zak the Yak with Books on His Back

Zak the Yak and His New Friend Quack

Praise for *Leaving Microsoft to Change the World*

"A rare business book that not only provides savvy insights for better business practices, but transcends the category altogether, to rank as an infectiously inspiring read...Marked by sincerity and savvy, this is the kind of book that business colleagues will discuss with their acquaintances, spouses and friend."

— *Publishers Weekly*, starred review

"Captivating....enlightening.....Wood [is an] exceptional writer."

— *Library Journal*

"I haven't cried so much reading a book in a long time. It's very emotional to read about both Wood's own struggles and the stories he tells of his travels. His outlook is wonderfully optimistic.

— Tom Peters, coauthor of the bestselling *In Search of Excellence*

"Always inspirational, this book is guaranteed to prompt many readers to open their hearts."

— *Booklist*

"Wood's dynamism permeates the book. The bottom line is passion, and it seems the world is better off for John Wood having followed his."

— *USA Today*

Made in the USA
Monee, IL
17 June 2020